THE M. & E. HANDBOOK SERIES

BUSINESS TYPEWRITING

THE M. & E. HANDBOOK SERIES

BUSINESS TYPEWRITING

SYLVIA F. PARKS
F.S.C.T., F.T.A., A.F.T.COM.

*Principal of The Camden Secretarial
Training School, Bath*

MACDONALD & EVANS LTD
8 John Street, London, WC1N 2HY

First published September 1972
Reprinted Febuary 1974
Reprinted September 1975

©

MACDONALD AND EVANS LIMITED
1972

ISBN: 0 7121 0230 2

This book is copyright and may not be reproduced in whole *or in part* (except for purposes of review) without the express permission of the publishers in writing.

HANDBOOK *Conditions of Sale*

This book is sold subject to the condition that it shall not, by way of *trade or otherwise*, be lent, resold, hired out or otherwise *circulated* without the publisher's prior consent in any form of binding or cover other than that in which it is published *and without a similar condition including this condition being imposed on the subsequent purchaser.*

Printed in Great Britain by
Butler & Tanner Ltd
Frome and London

PREFACE

THIS HANDBOOK describes the theory of typewriting layout and its practical application, and is intended as a revision book for examination candidates, or as a handy book of reference for the office typist. It does not try to teach anyone *how* to type, and it is assumed that the person using the book will have already mastered the keyboard and is able to type accurately at a reasonable speed.

This HANDBOOK shows how many forms of typewritten matter should be set out, with numerous diagrams and examples. It covers the syllabuses of *The Royal Society of Arts* Typewriting examinations at Elementary, Intermediate and Advanced stages, and of other examining bodies, such as Pitmans and the C.S.E.

In the facsimile typewriting illustrations the author has tried to give a general impression of the finished layout, as the text area available cannot accommodate the exact number of spaces a typist would use when typing on normal-sized paper.

Progress Tests follow each chapter and include a selection of actual past examination questions. The student is advised to use this HANDBOOK in conjunction with exercises from one of the many typewriting manuals available, and from questions appearing on past examination papers.

The author wishes to express her thanks to her sister, Mrs. Maureen Andrew, for help given with the typing of the manuscript, Mrs. M. J. Gay and Miss K. Wasson for the poetry examples, and *The Royal Society of Arts* for permission to reproduce questions from their past examination papers.

July 1972   S. F. P.

NOTICE TO LECTURERS

Many lecturers are now using **HANDBOOKS** as working texts to save time otherwise wasted by students in protracted note-taking. The purpose of the series is to meet practical teaching requirements as far as possible, and lecturers are cordially invited to forward comments or criticisms to the publishers for consideration.

P. W. D. REDMOND
General Editor

CONTENTS

CHAP.		PAGE
	PREFACE.	v
I.	The components and layout of a letter	
	1. Introduction	1
	2. Date	1
	3. Reference	1
	4. Inside name and address	2
	5. Salutation	5
	6. Heading	5
	7. Body of the letter	5
	8. Complimentary close	7
	9. Description of signatory	7
	10. Indication of enclosures	7
	11. Paragraphs	8
	12. Indented paragraph	9
	13. Block paragraph	9
	14. Hanging paragraph	10
	15. Typing an indented letter	10
	16. Typing a block letter	13
	17. Typing a semi-blocked letter	13
II.	Types of letters	
	1. Business letters	15
	2. Private letters	15
	3. Official letters	15
	4. Form letters	17
	5. Filling in forms	19
	6. Circulars	19
	7. Memoranda	21
	8. Envelope addressing	22
	9. Postcards	23
	10. Telegrams	23
III.	Manuscript work	
	1. Meaning of the word "manuscript"	27
	2. Reading the manuscript	27
	3. Correction signs	28
	4. Paragraphing	28
	5. Abbreviations	31

CHAP.		PAGE
III.	Manuscript work—*continued*	
	6. Words and figures	31
	7. Footnotes	34
	8. Technical manuscripts	35
	9. Typing from manuscript copy	37
IV.	Displayed work	
	1. General points about display	45
	2. Headings	45
	3. Underscoring	45
	4. Centring	46
	5. Tabular statements	46
	6. Line-spacing	46
	7. Ornamentation	46
	8. Some displayed documents	46
V.	Tabulation	
	1. General points about tabular work	57
	2. Leader dots	58
	3. Tables without ruling	59
	4. Tables with ruling	64
	5. Vertical headings	68
VI.	Commercial documents	
	1. A typical business transaction	75
	2. Enquiry	77
	3. Quotation, estimate and tender	78
	4. Order	80
	5. Delivery of goods and advice note	80
	6. Delivery and receipt note	81
	7. Invoice	82
	8. Credit and debit note	83
	9. Statement and payment	84
	10. Commercial abbreviations	84
VII.	Literary work	
	1. General points about literary work	88
	2. Quotation marks	91
	3. Estimating the length of a document	91
	4. Printer's proofs	91
	5. Plays	92
	6. Typing the play	93
	7. Actors' parts	98
	8. Programmes	99
	9. Poetry	101

CHAP.		PAGE
VIII.	Legal work	
	1. General rules	108
	2. Folding and endorsement	111
	3. Special clauses	113
	4. Types of legal document	113
	5. Legal abbreviations	114
IX.	Other business documents	
	1. General points about committee work	116
	2. Notices	116
	3. Agendas	118
	4. Minutes	119
	5. Specifications	121
	6. Bill of quantities	123
	7. Balance sheets	127
X.	Miscellaneous typewriting procedures	
	1. Division of words at line-endings	132
	2. Spacing after punctuation	133
	3. Time, money and quantities	133
	4. Hyphen and dash	134
	5. Combination signs	135
	6. Extra characters	135
	7. Roman numerals	138
	8. Ornamentation	139
	9. Types of paper	140
	10. Stationery sizes and uses	140
XI.	Copying and Duplicating	
	1. Methods of copying	143
	2. Carbon copying	143
	3. Ink duplicating	146
	4. Spirit duplicating	148
	5. Offset lithography	149
	6. Copying machines	150
XII.	Shorthand-typewriting and audio-typewriting	
	1. The shorthand-typist	153
	2. Receiving dictation	154
	3. Transcribing shorthand notes	154
	4. Audio-typewriting	155
	5. Transcribing recorded dictation	156
	6. Typing direct from dictation	156
	7. Other secretarial duties	156

CHAP.		PAGE
XIII.	Typewriting technique	
	1. Qualities of a competent typist	161
	2. Common typewriting errors	161
	3. Correction of errors	162
	4. Care of the typewriter	164
XIV.	Reference books	
	1. The need for reference books	168
	2. Reference books on English	168
	3. Telephone directories	169
	4. Street directories	169
	5. Post Office Guide	169
	6. Travel information	169
	7. Forms of address	170
	8. Dictionaries	170
	9. Other reference books	171

Appendixes

I.	Abbreviations	174
II.	Forms of address	180
III.	Examination technique	183
IV.	Examination papers	186

Index 191

LIST OF ILLUSTRATIONS

FIG.		PAGE
1.	The layout of an indented letter	2
2.	The layout of the continuation sheet of an indented letter	6
3.	The layout of a fully-blocked letter	8
4.	The layout of the continuation sheet of a fully-blocked letter	9
5.	The layout of a semi-blocked letter	10
6.	A business letter (indented method)	11
7.	A business letter (fully-blocked method, with open punctuation)	16
8.	The layout of a private letter	17
9.	The layout of an official letter	18
10.	A form letter.	20
11.	A memorandum	21
12.	The position of the address on an envelope	22
13.	A manuscript paragraph, with correction signs	32
14.	The same paragraph, correctly typed	33
15.	The position of a footnote in a typescript not intended for the printer	34
16.	The position of a footnote in a typescript intended for the printer	36
17.	A title page for a book	47
18.	A contents page for a book	48
19.	A contents page for a book, showing section headings	49
20.	A simple display for an advertisement	49
21.	A displayed handbill	50
22.	An application form	51
23.	An invitation	52
24.	A menu with a decorative border	53
25.	Rough plan of a tabular statement without ruling	60
26.	A completed table.	61
27.	Rough plan of a tabular statement with ruling	63
28.	Placing stencil dots before ruling	66
29.	A completed table.	67
30.	Part of a tabular statement, showing vertical headings	69
31.	A completed enquiry form	76
32.	A typical reply card	77

LIST OF ILLUSTRATIONS

FIG.		PAGE
33.	A quotation	78
34.	An order form	79
35.	An advice note	80
36.	A delivery note	81
37.	An invoice	82
38.	A credit note	83
39.	A debit note	84
40.	A statement	85
41.	Layout of the first page of a chapter	88
42.	Layout of the final page of a chapter, with a tail-piece	90
43.	The title page of a play	94
44.	A synopsis of Acts	95
45.	Characters and cast, with list of costumes	96
46.	The first page of a play	97
47.	An actor's part	98
48.	A concert programme	100
49.	Layout of the first page of a legal document	109
50.	Layout of the reverse page of a legal document	110
51.	An endorsement on a four-folded document	112
52.	A notice for a meeting	116
53.	An agenda, with centred items	117
54.	A Chairman's agenda	118
55.	Part of the first page of the minutes of a meeting	120
56.	Layout of an architect's or surveyor's specification	122
57.	Part of the first page of a bill of quantities	124
58.	A simple balance sheet	125
59.	A balance sheet with four money columns	126
60.	An itinerary	158

CHAPTER I

THE COMPONENTS AND LAYOUT OF A LETTER

1. Introduction. A letter can be divided into several parts, but not all of these are necessarily included in every type of letter. Letters almost always have the following parts:

(a) Date.
(b) Salutation.
(c) Body of the letter.
(d) Complimentary close.

Business letters usually have in addition the following parts:

(a) Reference.
(b) Inside name and address.
(c) Heading.
(d) Description of signatory.
(e) Indication of enclosures.

These parts are described in more detail in **2–10** below, but it must be borne in mind that individual firms often have a style and layout of their own.

2. Date. The date (*see* Fig. 1) may be written with or without punctuation, and, except in a fully-blocked letter, is usually placed at the top right-hand margin. The various ways of writing the date are listed below, but whatever style is chosen the order is always day, month and year, and it is never abbreviated:

1st January, 1973.	1 January, 1973.
1st January, 1973	1 January, 1973
1st January 1973	1 January 1973

NOTE: 1st, 2nd, etc., are never followed by a full stop.

3. Reference. There may be one or more references consisting of letters and/or numbers, but they usually comprise the initials of the person dictating the letter and the initials of the person typing the letter. These are written in capitals, with no punctuation and with an oblique line between the groups of letters, *e.g.* SGN/RB. The reference may be written

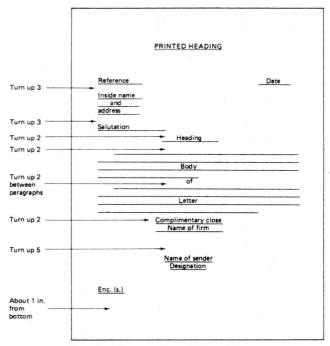

Fig. 1.—*Layout of an indented letter*

at the top or at the bottom of the page, at the left-hand margin, unless there is a special position marked on the paper for it. If there are two references, they are written underneath one another in single-spacing, and each may be preceded by either, "Your Ref." or "Our Ref.," and it is courteous to put the other person's reference first.

4. Inside name and address. This is the name and address of the person to whom the letter is being sent (the *addressee*), and when typing it, the following points should always be observed:

(*a*) Each part of the name and address should be written on a separate line and in single-line spacing, but if the address is rather long, the town and county may both be typed on the final line. It is best to accommodate the whole address on three lines, if possible.

(*b*) A comma is placed after each line, except the last, which has a full stop. If open punctuation is used, all commas and full stops are omitted (*see* **16**.).

(*c*) The name and address may be typed at the top or bottom of the page, according to the method of layout used, but it is always at the left-hand margin.

(*d*) Initials of Christian names are followed by a full stop (unless open punctuation is used), and they may be typed with or without a space in between, *e.g.* J. C. Smith, or J.C. Smith.

(*e*) The name and address can be written in an indented style:

John Smith, Esq.,
  16 High Street,
    Compton, Glos.

with each line indented $\frac{1}{2}$in., or in a block style:

John Smith, Esq.,
16 High Street,
Compton, Glos.

In this case, each line begins at the same point, and this is far more commonly used in general business letters than the indented form.

(*f*) There is no comma or full stop between the number and the name of the road. The town is only typed in capitals when a window envelope is to be used with the letter. When typing district numbers, leave one space, but no comma, after the name of the town and before the number, *e.g.* Bristol 4. If the district number contains letters and numbers, there is a comma and a space after the town, and full stops, but no spaces, between the letters and numbers, *e.g.* London, W.1.

(*g*) No abbreviations are allowed (*e.g.* "St." for Street, "Rd." for Road), except for some counties where the name is very long. The official abbreviations in all these cases are listed in *The Post Office Guide*.

(*h*) The postal code is written last, on a separate line and in capitals, *e.g.* BS16 6JJ.

(*i*) It is usual to add the courtesy title "Messrs." to the name of a firm if it is a partnership and not a limited company, *e.g.* Messrs. Smith & Brown; *but* Smith, Brown & Co., Ltd. should be used in the case of a limited company.

(*j*) The courtesy title "Esq." (meaning Esquire), is often used when writing to one man. It is used instead of "Mr.", and the two must never occur together, *e.g.* John Smith Esq., or Mr. John Smith. "Rev." (meaning Reverend), replaces "Mr." or "Esq." when writing to a clergyman. A full list of special forms of address is given in Appendix II.

(*k*) If the abbreviations "Jun." (meaning Junior) or "Sen." (meaning Senior) occur in the name, they are placed immediately after the name and before "Esq.," *e.g.* John Smith, Jun., Esq., *or* Mr. John Smith, Jun.

(*l*) Distinctions after a person's name are placed in the following order:

- (*i*) Decorations and honours, *e.g.* O.B.E.
- (*ii*) Educational qualifications, *e.g.* M.A.
- (*iii*) M.P. (Member of Parliament) and J.P. (Justice of the Peace).

A full stop is placed after each letter, and a comma and a space between each group of letters. V.C. takes precedence over all other decorations and honours.

EXAMPLE:
John Smith, Esq., O.B.E., M.A., M.P.

(*m*) If the inside name and address is that of a firm, but the letter is required to go to one particular person, it is usual to insert the phrase "For the attention of . . . ," followed by the name of that person. When typed, it is written at the left-hand margin, two line-spaces below the inside name and address, and is usually underlined. When a window envelope is to be used with the letter, the phrase should be written above the inside name and address—this is to comply with the Post Office regulation that nothing should appear under the postal code.

5. Salutation. The salutation (greeting) is varied, but the most common forms are: Dear Sir, Dear Madam, or Dear Mr. Smith. It always commences at the left-hand margin, and is followed by a comma unless open punctuation is used. The first letter of each word should be in capitals. There are special forms of address for persons of rank, such as a Baronet or an Archbishop; these are listed in Appendix II.

6. Heading. A heading is optional, but is often used to give the reader a preliminary idea of the contents of a letter. The following points should be observed when typing a heading:

(*a*) Its position varies according to the method of layout used. It may be either centred over the body of the letter, or typed at the left-hand margin. To centre a heading over the body:

- (*i*) Add the two numbers at which the margin stops are placed, and divide by two.
- (*ii*) Move the carriage as if to begin typing at that number on the paper bail scale.
- (*iii*) Back-space once for every two letters and spaces in the heading.
- (*iv*) Begin typing the heading at the point reached.

EXAMPLE:
To centre the heading "The Typewriter" with margins of 12 and 72:

- (*i*) $12 + 72 = 84; 84 \div 2 = 42$.
- (*ii*) Bring typewriting point to 42.
- (*iii*) Back-space seven times (for 13 letters + one space). The typewriting point is now at 35.
- (*iv*) Commence typing at this point.

(*b*) It may be written in capitals or lower case.

(*c*) If written in capitals, it is not usually underlined, but if written in lower case it is more effective when underlined.

(*d*) It is never followed by a full stop, unless the last word is an abbreviation.

(*e*) Punctuation marks are never underlined, unless they are in the middle of the heading.

7. Body of the letter. This is the main part of the letter, containing the message or information. There are several paragraph styles (*see* **11**, **12**, **13**, and **14**), but the following general points can be applied to any style:

(*a*) The paragraphs may be typed in single- or double-line spacing (according to the size of the letter), but whichever spacing is used, there is always double-line spacing between the paragraphs.

(*b*) All abbreviated words must be written in full, except recognised abbreviations such as *i.e.*, *e.g.*, *etc.*, *viz.*

(*c*) Although the right-hand margin should be kept as neat as possible, it is advisable not to divide words on more than two consecutive lines.

(*d*) The body of the letter may continue on to one or more pages, and if so, a plain sheet of paper is used for the continuation sheet. Each sheet is headed with the name of the person to whom the letter is being sent, the date, and the number of the page (*see* Figs. 2 and 4).

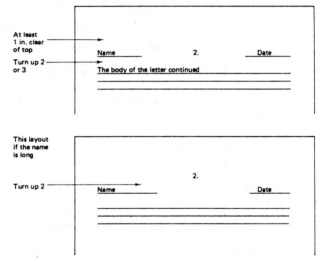

Fig. 2.—*Layout of the continuation sheet of an indented letter*

(*e*) If a continuation sheet is used, the last line on the first page should finish about 1 in. from the bottom.

(*f*) The last line of a paragraph should not be taken on

to a separate page, and a new paragraph should not be commenced at the bottom of a page, if only one line of it can be typed.

(*g*) The last word of a paragraph, or the last word on a page, should not be divided.

8. Complimentary close. The most usual ways of closing a letter are as follows:

(*a*) *Yours faithfully:* used in a business letter, where the salutation is "Dear Sir (Madam)."

(*b*) *Yours sincerely:* used in business or private letters if the salutation is less formal, *e.g.* "Dear Mr. Brown."

(*c*) *Yours truly:* used for business letters, where the salutation is "Dear Sir (Madam)." This is slightly less formal than (*a*).

Only the Y of "Yours" is capitalised in each case. The close is generally followed by a comma, but the position varies according to the layout adopted. There are special complimentary closes used with the special salutations. These are listed in Appendix II. Sometimes the name of the firm is placed under the complimentary close, in which case it is typed immediately under it, in single-line spacing, and often in block capitals.

9. Description of signatory. This is optional, but when it is used, it is placed below the complimentary close, after leaving five line-spaces clear for the signature. The name of the person signing the letter may also be typed, and if both a description, also called a designation, *e.g.* Chief Buyer, and name are required, the name is written first and the description immediately below (single-line spacing).

10. Indication of enclosures. There are several ways of indicating enclosures, but the most usual is to type the word "Enclosure(s)," or its abbreviation "Enc.(s.)" at the foot of the page, at the left-hand margin. It may be underlined if desired, and should be below the description of the signatory and at least 1 in. from the bottom of the page. If only a small portion of a continuation sheet has been used, the "Enc." may be as much as 2 or 3 in. from the bottom, in order to give the page a "balanced" look.

11. Paragraphs. All letters, whether business, private or official, use various types of paragraphing, which may be listed as follows:

(a) Indented paragraphs (*see* **12**).
(b) Block paragraphs (*see* **13**).
(c) Hanging paragraphs (*see* **14**).

Paragraphs may be used in different ways, in order to display the subject-matter most effectively. Letter layouts are given names according to the way in which the main paragraphs are typed, *e.g.* an *indented letter* has indented paragraphs (*see* Fig. 1.) a *block letter* has block paragraphs (*see* Fig. 3) and a *semi-blocked*

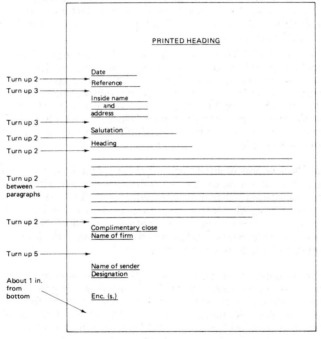

Fig. 3.—*Layout of a fully-blocked letter*

letter has block paragraphs, but an indented letter layout (*see* Fig. 5).

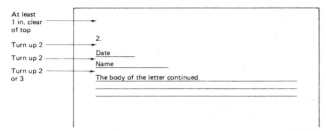

Fig. 4.—*Layout of the continuation sheet of a fully-blocked letter*

Sub-paragraphs and displayed paragraphs are often inset, and can be typed in a style different to that of the main paragraphs, *e.g.* indented main paragraphs with block sub-paragraphs. When inset, they are always typed in single-line spacing, and either indented equally from each margin, or indented from the left-hand margin only.

12. Indented paragraph. The indented paragraph is the one most commonly used in Britain for any kind of written matter. The first line is indented about $\frac{1}{2}$ in. from the left-hand margin (five spaces in, when using pica type; six spaces in, when using élite type). All subsequent lines begin at the margin, as shown below:

>   The practice of indenting the first line of
>   a paragraph is considered to be old-fashioned by
>   some people, but there are still many business
>   firms using this style in their correspondence.

13. Block paragraph. The block paragraph is gradually replacing the indented paragraph in general business use, as it is considered easier and quicker to type. The block paragraph is always typed in single-line spacing (with double-line spacing between paragraphs), and all lines begin at the same point, as shown below:

>   The block paragraph has been used in America
>   for general correspondence for many years and,
>   although the Continental firms have also been
>   using this style for some time, it is probable
>   that it originated in America.

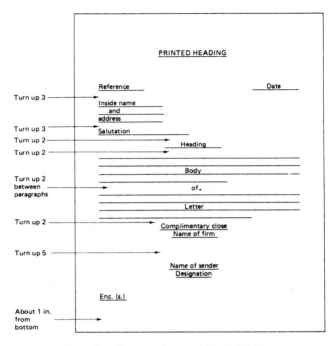

Fig. 5.—*Layout of a semi-blocked letter*

14. Hanging paragraph. The hanging paragraph is used principally for displaying information clearly, especially in sub-paragraphs, and usually occurs in conjunction with indented main paragraphs. It is also the accepted form of layout in certain documents, *e.g.* some kinds of specification. The first line begins at the normal point of typing, and all subsequent lines are indented two or three spaces, as shown below:

> The hanging paragraph is not used a great deal,
>   but it is useful inasmuch as it gives a neat
>   appearance and a certain emphasis to listed
>   sub-paragraphs.

15. Typing an indented letter. The following points should be noted:

SMITH, BROWN & CO.

BRISTOL

Ref. SGN/RB   10th October, 19--

J. C. Marden, Esq.,
19 Grove Road,
Compton Town.
GL4 19P

Dear Sir,

Central Heating Equipment

    We thank you for your enquiry, and it is with pleasure that we enclose our latest catalogue, with a price list and order form.

    Now that the winter is approaching, our goods are in great demand and we must point out that, to be sure of no delay in delivery of the goods, any order from you should be placed with us within the next two weeks.

                        Yours faithfully,
                      for SMITH, BROWN & CO.

                        Sales Manager

Enc.

FIG. 6.—*A business letter (indented method)*

(a) *The date* (*see* Fig. 6) is typed at the right-hand margin, two or three line-spaces below the printed heading. The back-spacer may be used (starting at the right-hand margin and allowing one space for each character in the date) in order to find the correct place to commence typing.

(*b*) *The reference* is typed exactly opposite the date, at the left-hand margin. If there are two references, the lower one should be opposite the date.

(*c*) *The inside name and address* is typed at the left-hand margin, usually three line-spaces below the reference. It may be typed in block or indented form, although the former is more usual (*see* **4** (*e*)).

Some business firms prefer the inside name and address to be typed at the foot of the letter; in this case, the last line finishes about 1 in. from the bottom of the page, and the "Enc.," if required, is placed two line-spaces above the name.

(*d*) *The salutation*, followed by a comma, is typed at the left-hand margin, three line-spaces below the inside name and address.

(*e*) *The heading* is typed two line-spaces below the salutation, and is centred over the body of the letter.

(*f*) *The body* of the letter is typed in indented paragraphs, but sub-paragraphs may be in the block or hanging styles.

(*g*) *The complimentary close* should begin two line-spaces below the end of the body, either centred or beginning approximately half-way across the page. If the name of the firm is required, it is typed immediately below the complimentary close (single-line spacing), and may be centred under, or begin at the same point as, the close.

(*h*) *Five line-spaces* are left clear for the signature.

(*i*) *The name of the sender* (if required), and the description of the signatory, are then typed below one another (single-line spacing), and may be centred under, or begin at the same point as, the close.

(*j*) *Indication of enclosures* is typed approximately 1 in. from the bottom of the page, at the left-hand margin.

(*k*) *Continuation sheets* are started about 1 in. from the top. The name of the person to whom the letter is being sent is written at the left-hand margin, the page number in the middle, and the date at the right-hand margin. The page number may be written as 2, 2., (2) or – 2 –. The typing then recommences two or three line-spaces below.

(*l*) *The margins* will vary according to the length of the letter, but 1 in.—2 in. is usual for the left-hand side, and

½ in.—1½ in. at the right-hand side. The right-hand margin must never be larger than the left-hand margin.

16. Typing a block letter. In a block letter, all the paragraphs are blocked, and every line commences at the left-hand margin, but the order in which the parts of the letter are typed are the same as in the indented method. This layout is easy and quick to type, but care must be taken with the margins, in order to avoid a lopsided effect. The advocates of the block letter layout often recommend the "open" method of punctuation; this is where all punctuation marks are omitted, except those essential to preserve the meaning in the body of the letter. In practice, this means that there is no punctuation in the date, the inside name and address, the salutation and the complimentary close; and frequently abbreviations do not have their customary full stops, *e.g.* UNESCO (*see* Fig. 7).

17. Typing a semi-blocked letter. This layout is a cross between the indented method and the block method. The letter is set out exactly as in the indented method, but block instead of indented paragraphs are used in the body of the letter. Headings of continuation sheets are the same as in the indented method (*see* Fig. 4).

PROGRESS TEST 1

1. List the parts of a letter. (**1**)
2. Describe the position and method of typing the reference in a letter. How would you type two references? (**3**)
3. (*a*) What is the "inside address"?
    (*b*) Describe the most common methods of typing the inside address. (**4**)
4. When should the title "Messrs." be used? (**4**)
5. If the abbreviation "Jun." appears in a name, should "Esq." be typed before or after it? (**4**)
6. "Yours faithfully" and "Yours sincerely" are two methods of finishing a letter. When might each of these be used? (**8**)
7. What is the "description," as used in a letter? (**9**)
8. Name and describe the three main types of paragraphing used when typing correspondence. (**11–14**)
9. When using the indented method of layout for a letter:

(a) At which margin is the date typed?

(b) How many line-spaces are left clear above and below the inside address?

(c) What style of paragraphing would be used for the main paragraphs in the body of the letter?

(d) Why are several line-spaces left clear underneath the complimentary close?

(e) If a continuation sheet is required, how would the beginning of that page be set out? (**15**)

10. What is "open" punctuation? (**16**)

11. What are the main points of difference between the indented and block methods of laying out a letter? (**15, 16**)

12. What is the difference between the indented method and the semi-blocked method of laying out a letter? (**15, 17**)

CHAPTER II

TYPES OF LETTERS

1. Business letters. Business letters may be set out in any of the ways described in Chapter I (*i.e.* indented, block or semi-blocked) and are usually typed on the firm's headed notepaper which can be any size, depending on what is most suitable for its business. Less formal business letters, especially if commencing with "Dear Mr. Smith," for example, and finishing with "Yours sincerely," may have the inside name and address written at the end of the letter instead of above the salutation. In this case, the last line of the address would finish about 1 in. from the bottom of the page, and "Enc." would be two or three line-spaces above the name.

2. Private letters. Private (or personal) letters differ principally in the fact that headed notepaper of a firm is not generally used, and the typist types the sender's address at the top right-hand corner of the paper. This address is usually typed in indented form, and the last line should finish at the margin. To find where to commence the address, back-space from the right-hand margin (back-spacing a sufficient number of spaces in order adequately to accommodate the address). The date is written two line-spaces below the final line, at the right-hand margin. The letter then continues in the same way as for a business letter, but it is usual to type the inside address (if it is used) at the bottom of the page, as is done for a less formal business letter (*see* Fig. 8).

3. Official letters. Official letters are those sent from government departments, and until quite recently they were written in a very formal style. The style now being used is much more like that of an ordinary business letter, but it differs in the following ways:

(*a*) Below the printed letter-head are two parallel lines. Within these are typed the inside name and address and references, on the left, and the date, on the right.

(b) The block method of layout, and open punctuation, is used.

```
           S M I T H ,   B R O W N   &   C O .

                       B R I S T O L



10 October 19--

Ref SGN/RB


J C Marden Esq
19 Grove Road
Compton Town
GL4 19P


Dear Sir

Central Heating Equipment

We thank you for your enquiry, and it is with pleasure
that we enclose our latest catalogue, with a price list
and order form.

Now that the winter is approaching, our goods are in great
demand and we must point out that, to be sure of no delay
in delivery of the goods, any order from you should be
placed with us within the next two weeks.

Yours faithfully
for SMITH BROWN & CO



Sales Manager




Enc
```

FIG. 7.—*A business letter (fully-blocked method, with open punctuation)*

(c) A common salutation (*e.g.* "Dear Sir") will normally be used, but in more formal letters the salutation is "Sir" or "Sirs."

(d) The complimentary close is the same as for business letters, but in more formal letters the style may be either, "I am, Sir, Your obedient Servant;" or, "I have the honour to be, Sir, Your obedient Servant."

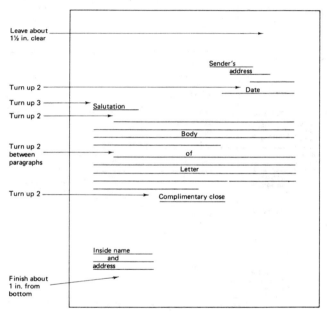

FIG. 8.—*Layout of a private letter*

(e) When more than one page is required, the typing continues on the reverse side of the paper, commencing where the first line of the body of the letter began on the first side.

(f) Continuation sheets are headed with the name of the addressee, the date and the page number, as in a blocked business letter (*see* Fig. 9).

4. Form letters. A form letter is one which has a typed

form at the end, which may be torn off and used as a reply. When typing a form letter, the following points should be observed:

(a) The dotted lines are double-spaced. This allows plenty of room for them to be filled in.

(b) The number of line-spaces required for the form must be carefully estimated, before commencing to type the letter.

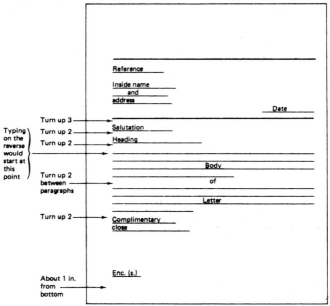

FIG. 9.—*Layout of an official letter*

Allow at least three clear spaces below the line dividing the letter from the form, and about 1 in. clear at the bottom of the page.

(c) Having estimated the amount of space required for the form, arrange the letter appropriately on the remainder of the page. (A light pencil mark, which is rubbed out afterwards, may be used to indicate where the dividing line will occur; this will help when arranging the letter, and when the paper is actually in the typewriter.)

(d) The dotted lines must be lightly typed.

(e) One clear space must be left before and after any typewriting which may occur with the dotted lines (*see* Fig. 10).

5. Filling in forms. When typewriting a reply on a form, the procedure is as follows:

(a) Insert the form in the machine, and using the variable line-spacer, line up the dotted lines at the normal line of typewriting.

(b) Again using the variable line-spacer, lower the dotted lines so that any typewriting will be slightly above the dots, as illustrated below. This will prevent the typewriting from merging with the dots.

.........The.typewriting.is.raised.above.the.dots:......

(c) Type in the normal way; if the dotted lines are so spaced that they do not correspond with the line-spacing of the typewriter, it will be necessary to re-align each new line of typing.

6. Circulars. Circular letters are usually printed or duplicated, but the typist may be required to prepare the copy. Any layout may be used, but a circular letter will differ from an ordinary business letter in the following way:

(a) The date often consists of the month and year only.

(b) The inside name and address is omitted, but where this normally occurs, a space large enough for a long name and address is left clear. This is so that the typist (or an automatic typewriter with address plates) can insert the name and address after the letter has been printed.

(c) If a person's name is required in the salutation, the only word to appear in the copy is "Dear." No comma follows. As with the inside name and address, the name is inserted later by the typist. If "Dear Sir" or "Dear Madam" is to be used, this would be typed on the copy in the usual way before sending it to the printer.

(d) The original signature does not usually occur on each letter if there is a large number of circulars to be sent out; instead, the typist types in the name of the sender. This is positioned three line-spaces below the complimentary close, and three line-spaces above the designation. The printer might use a block to produce a facsimile signature when the letters are printed.

```
                    S M I T H ,   B R O W N   &   C O .

                              B R I S T O L

                                                  10th October, 19--

The Owner,
19 Grove Road,
Compton Town,
GL4 19P


Dear Sir,

        We are taking this opportunity to inform you of our
new-style central heating equipment.  All our goods are
now manufactured at our own works, and are sold under the
brand name BROWNSMITH.

        If you are thinking of installing central heating
in your home, why not fill up the attached form, and we
shall be pleased to forward our catalogue and price list.

                                  Yours faithfully,



                                  Sales Manager

................................................................


   To:   Smith, Brown & Co.,
         Bristol.


   Please forward your catalogue and price list to:


   Name .......................................................
   Address ....................................................
              ................................................
```

FIG. 10.—*A form letter*

II. TYPES OF LETTERS

7. Memoranda. Memoranda, often called "memos" for short, are used for interdepartmental communication within a firm, and are typed as follows (*see* Fig. 11):

(*a*) Printed memo sheets are generally used, but if they are not available, A5-size paper may be used lengthwise

M E M O R A N D U M

To: All Departments   Date: 1st December, 19--

From: The Manager   Ref: PM/HOL

Christmas Holidays

Will employees please note that as Christmas Day falls on
a Friday, Saturday (26th December) is the official Bank
holiday, and everyone will be expected to return to work
at 9 a.m. on Monday, 28th December.

FIG. 11.—*A memorandum*

(*i.e.* with the typewriting parallel to the longest edge); if the message is lengthy, A4-size paper may be used the normal way up (*i.e.* with the typewriting parallel to the shortest edge).

(*b*) The paper is headed with the word MEMORANDUM, which, if not already printed, is typed in spaced capitals, (*see* Fig. 11).

(*c*) Three line-spaces beneath this are printed (or typed) the following: *To . . ., From . . ., Ref. . . ., Date . . .*, and the typist fills in the appropriate names, etc. in each space.

(*d*) There is no inside address, salutation, complimentary close or signature, although the names of the departments of both the sender and the recipient may be typed (in addition to their own names), and the sender may sometimes initial the memo after it is typed.

(*e*) Sometimes a ruled line separates the headings from the message.

(*f*) The body of the memo may have a heading, in which case it is typed in the same manner as a heading over the body of a letter. Indented or block paragraphs may be used when typing the main part of the memo.

8. Envelope addressing. The following points should be observed when addressing envelopes:

(*a*) The name and address may be typed in indented or block form, but the style is usually the same as that used for the inside name and address on the original letter. If, however, the envelope is large, the indented form is used, with double-line spacing instead of single-line spacing; for extra-large envelopes, treble-line spacing may even be employed. The envelope must be of suitable size and quality to take the letter and any enclosures without undue folding.

(*b*) Always type the name and address parallel to the longest side of the envelope.

(*c*) If an envelope with a flap at the side is used, the flap should be on the right-hand side of the typed address.

(*d*) Start typing slightly over half-way down the envelope (*see* Fig. 12); the name and address as a whole should be centred horizontally, with each item on a separate line (it is not necessary to use only three lines).

(*e*) The rules regarding the typing of an inside name and address should be followed (*see* I, **4**), except that the town

```
            Personal

            J. C. Marden, Esq.,
            19 Grove Road,
            COMPTON TOWN,
            Glos.
            GL4 19P
```

FIG. 12.—*The position of the address on an envelope*

should be typed in capitals, and double- or treble-line spacing may be used, as stated in (*a*) above.

(*f*) Additional words and phrases, such as "Personal," "Urgent," "For the attention of . . ." or "Confidential" may be typed either two line-spaces above the name, or in the bottom left-hand corner of the envelope. These words are underlined, and must not be written at the top of the envelope as they might be obliterated by Post Office franking.

(*g*) Nothing must be typed or written under the postal code, which is always typed in capitals.

9. Postcards. It is usual for a firm to have postcards with a printed heading, containing their name, address and other details; when typing these there is no inside name and address, salutation, or complimentary close. Apart from this, they are typed in the same manner as business letters—on one side only, and with the name and address of the addressee on the reverse. If the message is fairly long, the margins may be of three or four spaces only, and the typing may extend much closer to the bottom edge of the card than is normal; for this purpose, most typewriters have a special card-holding attachment.

10. Telegrams. When preparing a telegram, it must be remembered that the message has to be kept as concise as possible, although the meaning must still be quite clear. All words and punctuation in the message and the address will be charged for, so if the telegraphic address is known it should be used.

When typing a telegram the following points should be observed:

(*a*) Use the correct telegram form, as supplied by the Post Office.

(*b*) Use block capitals throughout.

(*c*) Leave two or three spaces between each word.

(*d*) Avoid using any punctuation. At the end of a sentence type "STOP"—the charge for a punctuation mark is the same as if it were written as a word, and a written word is much clearer than a dot.

(*e*) A telegram should be confirmed by a letter sent at the same time, if possible.

PROGRESS TEST 2

1. How does a private or personal letter differ from a business letter? (**2**)

2. How does an official letter differ from a business letter? (**3**)

3. (*a*) When typing a form or a form letter, why are the dotted lines double-spaced? (**4**)

    (*b*) What are the points to be borne in mind when typing dotted lines? (**4**)

4. When filling up a form, why must the typewriting be slightly raised above the dotted lines? (**5**)

5. Describe the layout of a circular letter? (**6**)

6. Describe the layout of a memorandum, assuming no headed memo sheets are available. (**7**)

7. (*a*) When addressing an envelope, the most usual method is to type the name and address in block form. When might the indented form be used? (**8**)

    (*b*) How does the name and address on an envelope differ from the inside name and address? (**8**)

8. When typing additional wording on an envelope (such as "Personal" or "Urgent") why must it not be typed at the top of the envelope? What is the best position for these words? (**8**)

9. What parts of a business letter are omitted when typing a postcard? (**9**)

The Elementary, Intermediate and Advanced Typewriting questions in the following Progress Tests are all reproduced by kind permission of the Royal Society of Arts, as are those in Appendix IV. The level and year is printed beneath each question.

II. TYPES OF LETTERS

Please type one copy of the following form on plain white paper.

SUGGESTED DRAFT FORM

<u>PENSION/LIFE ASSURANCE SCHEME</u>

SURNAME . . . .

FIRST NAMES . . . .

ADDRESS . . . .

. . . .

DATE OF BIRTH . . . .

DEPARTMENT . . . .

SALARY . . . .

YEARS OF SERVICE . . . .

NEXT OF KIN :— Surname . . . .
                First Names . . . .
                Address . . . .
                . . . .

I wish my contributions to be deducted from salary :—
      monthly / quarterly / annually *

Signature . . . . Date . . . .

* Please delete as appropriate.

On the appropriate paper type a copy of the memorandum for despatch today from B. Phillips to H. Turner. Take 2 carbon copies on yellow paper. Type the following in the top left-hand corner of one of the carbon copies - <u>For the attention of Mrs. M. Raynor</u>

Office Practice Classes

In view of my admission to hospital next week, I now enclose outline notes for the office practice lessons which I had planned for the following 2 weeks. I think these will be sufficient for my substitute, Mrs. M. Raynor, for the period of my absence. The students have not covered any of these subjects during the current session, so Mrs. R. can extend within these notes on as wide a theme as she wishes.

If there is any time to spare the students can use any of the machines in the Office Appliance Centre. There are several spirit duplicating masters to be run off + the students are capable of working in the Centre with the minimum of supervision.

I am working on the 'mock' exam. papers + hope to let you have these by the end of this week.

R.S.A.—ELEMENTARY 1971

CHAPTER III

MANUSCRIPT WORK

1. Meaning of the word "manuscript." According to the dictionary, the word "manuscript" means any document written by hand, *i.e.* not printed, and this obviously includes any handwritten business documents such as letters, tabulations or anything else which the typist is required to copy. This chapter deals mainly with the manuscript reports and other more lengthy general documents which comprise the "manuscript" question in most typewriting examinations, but many of the points mentioned apply to any manuscript work.

Legal and literary manuscripts are dealt with in later chapters.

2. Reading the manuscript. The typist must read through the whole document (or at least several pages of it) before commencing to type. The main reasons for this are as follows:

(*a*) It will give an idea of the contents, which makes the typing easier.

(*b*) It will help the typist to estimate the length of the document, and she can then have the necessary amount of paper at hand.

(*c*) It enables the typist to get used to the style of writing. This is especially important for deciphering difficult or badly written words, although sometimes, even after reading to the end, there may be a word that is still not clear. If this happens, the best plan is to compare an individual letter in the word in question with what appears to be a similar letter in another, more legible word. Repeat this process for the other letters in the illegible word and it will probably become clear. If it is still not recognisable, the writer of the document must be asked. If the writer is not available, a blank space of appropriate length must be left in the typescript. On no account must the typist guess a word.

(*d*) Any queries concerning spellings can be checked with a dictionary.

(*e*) Suspected grammatical errors must be queried with the writer; if he is not available the errors may be corrected; if there is any doubt concerning these, a book such as Fowler's *Modern English Usage* can be referred to.

(*f*) If necessary, unusual or unfamiliar technical terms may be checked with the writer before the commencement of typing. If all the queries concerning the document are listed on a sheet of paper, it will necessitate only one interview, and so save the time of both writer and typist.

(*g*) Pencil notes may be lightly written in the margin. Such notes will probably concern the layout, the emphasising of special instructions and correction signs, spellings, abbreviations, etc.

3. Correction signs. The writer may use correction signs in the margin, indicating that he wishes to change the original manuscript in some way (*see* Fig. 13). The following correction signs are commonly used, but they are not the same in every case as the correction signs used by printers. The different signs printers use are discussed fully in Chapter VII. Fig. 14 shows a typed paragraph after all corrections have been done.

4. Paragraphing. Main paragraphs must all be of the same style (usually indented or block paragraphs), and are normally typed in double-line spacing. Sub-paragraphs may be inset, in which case they are typed in single-line spacing and, as in a letter, they may be of a style different to that of the main paragraphs, *e.g.* blocked sub-paragraphs with indented main paragraphs. Use double-line spacing between all paragraphs.

The paragraphs may be numbered, and the following rules apply if numbering is required:

(*a*) The main paragraphs are usually numbered with arabic figures (1, 2, 3, etc.).

(*b*) The sub-paragraphs may be numbered with arabic figures (if these have not been used for the main paragraphs), small letters of the alphabet ((a), (b), (c), etc.), or small roman numerals ((i), (ii), (iii), etc.). If sub-paragraphs are divided into separate points, use the small letters for the

III. MANUSCRIPT WORK

Typists' Correction Signs

Correction sign		Meaning	Interpretation
In margin	In text		
	Word(s) underlined once		Underscore the word(s)
Caps	Word(s) underlined twice	Capitals	Type the word(s) underlined in block capitals. Do not underscore unless asked.
Sp. Caps	Word(s) underlined three times	Spaced capitals	Type the word(s) underlined in spaced capitals, i.e. one clear space between each letter and three clear spaces between each word. Not usually underscored.
u.c.	Mark under letter(s)	Upper case	Change to a capital letter(s), where marked.
l.c.	Mark under letter(s)	Lower case	Change to a small letter(s), where marked.
N.P.	Square bracket or two lines at the beginning of word(s)	New paragraph	Commence a new paragraph at the marked word.
run on	A connecting line between two paragraphs	Run on	Do not commence a new paragraph or word — join the two paragraphs together.
trs.	A mark embracing several letters or words	Transpose	Change the order of the letters or words — the individual words or letters may be numbered to indicate the new order.
stet	Dotted line (...) under letter(s) or word(s)	Let it stand — i.e. leave as originally written	A letter or word which has been crossed out must not now be changed. It must be written as it appeared before the crossing-out. (Sometimes there may be several crossed-out words written above one another — the word with the dotted line underneath is the one to be typed. See Fig. 13.)

Typists' Correction Signs

Correction sign		Meaning	Interpretation
In margin	In text		
↳/ or ↲	A word(s) or letter(s) crossed through	Delete	Delete the word(s) or letter(s) crossed through.
⊙	Omission mark	Full stop	Insert full stop at point marked in text.
, or ⸴	Omission mark	Comma	Insert comma at point marked in text.
/-/	Omission mark	Hyphen	Insert hyphen at point marked in text.
#	Omission mark	Space	Insert space at point marked in text.
' or ⸲	Omission mark	Apostrophe	Insert apostrophe at point marked in text.
ʼʼ or ⸲⸲	Omission mark	Quotation marks	Insert quotation marks at point marked in text.
	⌐┘		Move line(s) to the left.
	└¬		Move line(s) to the right.
//	Mark beside edge of typewriting		Straighten alignment of margin.
⌒	⌒ between letters	Close up	Move letters closer together.

sub-paragraphs and the roman numerals for the individual points.

(*c*) All numbers and letters may be either followed by a full stop, or bracketed. Two spaces are left clear after the full stop or bracket.

(*d*) Units should always appear under units, *e.g.*

   8.
   9.
  10.

(*e*) Roman numerals should be lined up from the right, *e.g.*

    i.
    ii.
    iii.

(*f*) Whichever method of numbering is adopted, care must be taken to ensure uniformity throughout the whole document.

5. Abbreviations.

Many abbreviations occur in manuscripts and most must be rendered in full. Some, however, may be typed as abbreviations, for example: *et seq., e.g., i.e., etc., viz., N.B., Mr., Mrs., Messrs., Esq.*

The following may be typed as abbreviations when they occur in the name of a firm: *Co., Bros., &, Ltd.*

If occurring before the name of a ship, *s.s.* may be left as an abbreviation.

In Appendix I is a list of some abbreviations likely to be found written in a general manuscript.

6. Words and figures. When typing documents from manuscript, it is necessary, in some cases, to render figures in words. The following general rules may be applied, but the typist must always follow any special instructions concerning the use of words instead of figures.

(*a*) *Use words instead of figures:*

    (*i*) For numbers one to nine, inclusive, in general matter. For numbers one to one hundred, and round numbers over one hundred, in literary matter.
    (*ii*) When a sentence begins with a number.
    (*iii*) For approximate numbers, and when ordinal numbers (*i.e.* first, second, etc.) are used for ages or centuries.
    (*iv*) For time, when preceding "o'clock."
    (*v*) When referring to population when a round number is being expressed.
    (*vi*) For streets taking numbers as names, *i.e.* Forty-second Street, Fifth Avenue.
    (*vii*) For legal or other official matter where accuracy is essential.

caps.	Manuscript work ⟶ centre
⊙ u/c l :	[I]/R the meaning of the word "manuscript"/
run on l,	(According to the dictionary/the word "manuscript" means any
l,	document written by hand/i.e. not printed, and this
tr.	includes obviously any handwritten business documents such
Stet	as letters, tabulations, or ~~anything~~ _something_ else which the typist is
l.c.	required to copy. This Chapter deals mainly with
	manuscript reports and other more lengthy general documents
[,],	which comprise the/manuscript/question in most typewriting
⌐	examinations, but much of the ~~following~~ information can
N.P.	apply to any manuscript work. ⌈Legal and literary ~~manu~~
	scripts are dealt with in later chapters.

FIG. 13.—*A manuscript paragraph, with correction signs*

MANUSCRIPT WORK

1. The meaning of the word "manuscript": According to the dictionary, the word "manuscript" means any document written by hand, i.e. not printed, and this obviously includes any handwritten business documents such as letters, tabulations, or anything else which the typist is required to copy. This chapter deals mainly with manuscript reports and other more lengthy general documents which comprise the "manuscript" question in most typewriting examinations, but much of the information can apply to any manuscript work.

Legal and literary scripts are dealt with in later chapters.

FIG. 14.—*The same paragraph, correctly typed*

(b) *Use figures instead of words:*

   (i) For numbers ten and over in general matter; for numbers over one hundred, except round numbers, in literary matter.
   (ii) When referring to quantities, measurements, sums of money, dates, house numbers, district numbers and degrees of temperature.
   (iii) Before the abbreviations a.m. and p.m.

7. Footnotes. It may be necessary to include one or more footnotes; these are typed in the following manner:

(a) The footnote sign, which may be a figure, asterisk, dagger or double dagger (*see* X, **5**), is typed immediately after, and is raised half a space above, the word or phrase in the main text to which the note refers, *e.g.* "Many years ago*they...."

(b) The footnotes are typed at the bottom of the page on which the reference mark occurs. Footnotes should not run over on to two pages.

(c) A continuous line is typed across the page, separating the main text from the footnote. One clear line-space is left either side of the line.

(d) Footnotes are always typed in single-line spacing (*see* Fig. 15). One space is left clear between the sign and the first word.

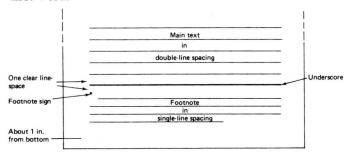

FIG. 15.—*The position of a footnote in a typescript not intended for the printer*

(e) The last line of typing in the footnote should finish 1 in. from the bottom of the page.

(*f*) If there is more than one footnote, one clear line-space is left between each note.

(*g*) The space required for the footnotes must be calculated as the typing progresses down the page. Estimate the number of lines required for the note; add two extra line-spaces (one for the space above the dividing line, one for the space below the dividing line), and 1 in. (six line-spaces) for the clear space at the bottom of the page. Measure this total distance from the bottom of the page and, if possible, mark it lightly with a pencil—this will indicate when to begin the spacing for the footnote. If it is not possible to mark the page like this, the part already used can be measured and then it will be possible to estimate the amount of clear space left; if there is one, the fixed ruler on the typewriter may also be used. Occasionally, words requiring footnotes occur near the bottom of a page. If this happens, it might be difficult to estimate beforehand the space required. Great care must therefore be taken when typing near the bottom of the sheet if a footnote word is likely to appear.

(*h*) When preparing a typescript for the printer, the footnote is *not* typed at the bottom of the page (*see* Fig. 16). The actual typing is the same as above (*i.e.* single-line spacing, etc.), but the footnote is positioned immediately under the line of typing to which it refers. Dividing lines are typed above and below the footnote, separating it from the main text, and one space is left above and below each line. The main text then continues on the next line.

8. Technical manuscripts. Some manuscript work may be of a highly technical nature and contain such things as mathematical equations, chemical formulae, and long unusual words. Great care must be taken with the typing and checking of these manuscripts, and the following points should be noted:

(*a*) Superior characters are those raised slightly above the normal line of typing, and inferior characters are those dropped slightly below it. These often occur in mathematical and chemical formulae, and when typing them the variable line-spacer may be used to raise or lower the point of

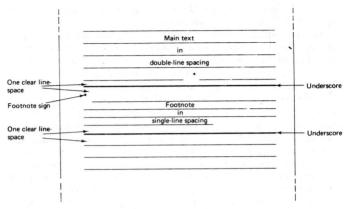

FIG. 16.—*The position of a footnote in a typescript intended for the printer*

typing, or the platen can be turned half a line-space up or down, *e.g.* H_2O, x^2.

(*b*) The addition sign (+) and the equals sign (=) are included on a normal keyboard; a small x can be used for the multiplication sign (×), a hyphen for the subtraction sign (—) and a hyphen and colon combined for the division sign (÷), if these are not on the typewriter. (*See* X, **5**.) Special typewriters are available if a large amount of mathematical work has to be done but if a special typewriter is not available mathematical signs such as the square root sign and the integral sign may be written in with black ink after the typing has been completed.

(*c*) When typing equations, leave one space before and after each sign, *e.g.* $x^2 + y^2 = 45 - 5y$. When an equation requires two or more line spaces, care must be taken to see that any writing occurring with it is aligned with the centre of the equation. If there are several rows of equations, one clear line-space must be left between the bottom line of the top equation and the top line of the bottom equation.

(*d*) There are a few common fractions on a normal keyboard, and these are used when they occur in the text; but if the fraction required is not on the keyboard, sloping fractions may be typed. This entails the use of the solidus (oblique), and if a whole number occurs with the fraction, a space must be left clear between the whole number and the first figure of the fraction, *e.g.* 10 5/6.

NOTE: There is no space between the whole number and the fraction when the complete fraction is already provided on the keyboard, *e.g.* 10½.

9. Typing from manuscript copy. The following additional points should be noted when typing a document:

(*a*) Read and follow any special instructions, *e.g.* the writer may not wish to have double-line spacing.

(*b*) If tabular work occurs in the body of the document, do any arithmetical calculations before commencing to type —this will help you to arrange the matter on the page most effectively.

(*c*) The typewriting commences 1 in. from the top of the page, and the usual margins are 1 in. at the left-hand side and ½ in. at the right-hand side.

(*d*) The first page is not numbered, but all following pages are numbered at the top, the figure being centred over the line of writing.

(*e*) Headings are displayed appropriately (*see* IV, **2–4**). Sub-headings may be either centred over the line of writing, or typed at the left-hand margin.

(*f*) If the document is typed with double-line spacing, two clear spaces (*i.e.* turn up three), are left between the heading and the body of the work. If single-line spacing is to be used, one clear space is left.

(*g*) Space for footnotes must be calculated *before* reaching the bottom of the page.

(*h*) The last line of typewriting on a page should be 1 in. from the bottom.

(*i*) The last line of a paragraph should not be taken on to a separate page, and a new paragraph should not be commenced at the bottom of a page if only one line of it can be typed.

(*j*) Read through each page before removing from the typewriter—it is much easier to correct any errors if the paper has not been removed.

(*k*) Type on one side of the paper only unless specially instructed.

(*l*) Make full use of the tabulator stop, *e.g.* stops for paragraph indentation, displayed paragraphs, numbering of paragraphs, etc. This will help to keep the layout consistent, which is a very important factor, as well as making the actual typing speedier.

(*m*) Take care with division of words at the ends of lines (*see* X, **1**).

(*n*) Make correct use of roman numerals in the text (*see* X, **7**), and render abbreviations in full (III, **5**).

PROGRESS TEST 3

1. Give reasons why it is necessary to read through a manuscript before commencing to type. (**2**)

2. Write the typists' correction signs for the following:

   (*a*) Lower case.
   (*b*) Delete.
   (*c*) Insert space.
   (*d*) Spaced capitals.
   (*e*) Move row to the left.
   (*f*) Leave as originally written. (**3**)

3. What is the most usual method of numbering sub-paragraphs? (**4**)

4. When typing from manuscript, most abbreviations must be rendered in full. Give eight abbreviations which are exceptions to this rule. (**5**)

5. In typing from manuscript copy, when are words used instead of figures? (**6**)

6. Describe how you would type a footnote for:

   (*a*) An author's copy.
   (*b*) A printer's copy. (**7**)

7. What are superior and inferior characters? (**8**)

8. How would you type a division sign, if it were not included on the keyboard? (**8**)

9. What are sloping fractions? Describe how they are typed. (**8**)

III. MANUSCRIPT WORK

Type one copy of the following on plain white paper.
No carbon copy is required.

Some of the services of the post office

CASH ON DELIVERY (or trade charge) – A cash amount
(not exceeding £50) specified by the sender for collection
on delivery can, under certain conditions, be collected by
the Post Office. This amount is then remitted to the sender
by means of a crossed order.

BUSINESS REPLY SERVICE – Under this service a person
wishing to obtain replies without putting the clients to
the expense of paying postage may enclose in their
communications an unstamped card, envelope, gummed label.
The postage, together with an additional fee on each item,
is paid by the addressee. A licence to use this service
must be obtained from the Post Office.

RAILEX – An unregistered packet can be taken to any
post office which is also an express delivery office for
conveyance to the railway station for despatch by the
next train. A messenger will meet the train and deliver
the packet. A prepaid telegram is sent to the post office
asking that the train be met and stating the time.

RAILWAY LETTERS – These are sent from the railway
station where they are handed in on the first available
train for transfer on arrival to the nearest post office,
or to be collected by a post office messenger who will
deliver the letter.

PHONOPOST – Spoken messages can be recorded on disc
or tape, and posted for dispatch abroad. All recordings
sent by this service must be enclosed in strong protective
covers.

(Further details are, of course, available in the
Post Office Guide and also in the various books in the
library. I suggest that homework be given for the
setting out of these services in more detail by reference
to the P.O. Guide.)

Type one copy of the following manuscript. Use double line spacing, except where otherwise indicated.

Spaced caps.
L I V I N G in a New House

6 years ago we reported on the experiences of over 1,500 Members who had bought new homes. The report did not, in general, make cheerful reading. Many members had been put to unexpected trouble or expense, in particular by:

u.c.

1. ~~the cost of modifications to the builder's basic design;~~
1. delays in the completion of building; and
2. straight increases in the builder's price before handing over. ~~and~~
~~having to carry out repairs as soon as they took the house over.~~

So we decided to look at the situation again — this time drawing on the experiences of 3 thousand Members who had recently moved into newly-built houses.

Closed caps.
1. Delays

In the earlier survey we found that only a ¼ of our members' houses were completed by the promised date. In this survey we found that more houses — about one in three — were completed on time; but those who were delayed had often to wait several months before they could move in. Out of every 100 delayed:

  39 waited one month or less
  27 waited about two months   ⎫
  23 waited three or four mths.   ⎬ → Centre in single line spacing.
  11   "   five months or more   ⎭

Only 2 out of every 100 got any compensation for the delay. Clearly, when you commit yourself to buy a new house while it is still being built, you cannot rely on being able to move in on the

III. MANUSCRIPT WORK

trs. date (promised) (originally). So if you are selling the house you are leaving, you should think twice about undertaking to leave by a certain date.

What causes delays?

We found ~~that~~ three factors which were related to the length of delay: ~~for our Members:~~
Time of year. Houses scheduled for completion in the spring + early summer (March to June) were more likely to be finished on time than other houses. Members expecting completed houses in the autumn, in general, suffered the longest delays.
Modifications. Members who had asked the builder for modifications waited longer for completion than Members who had not.
Who sells it. Members who had bought their houses directly from the builder were able to move in sooner than those who had bought new houses through estate agents.

2. PRICE INCREASES

Between the time you agree to buy, and the time the house is completed, the cost of labour or materials may rise or the weather may be unusually foul. In his contract with you, the builder may reserve the right to pass on to you
N.P. any additional costs such as these. [We do not think this is unreasonable, but suggest that in the contract you try to reserve the right to withdraw from negotiations - with return of any
stet deposit - if the price does ~~go up.~~
Run on (If you are asked to pay extra, your solicitor should be satisfied that the increase is legitimate.

Type the following in double line spacing. All abbreviations are to be rendered in full.

TELEVISION TRANSMISSION
TECHNICAL TERMS

Having dealt with the general principles of television transmission & reception, it is now necessary to consider in greater detail some of the technical terms.

Black & white picture

A form of distortion in which dark objects are outlined on the right-hand side by a white line. In its simple form, picture sharpness is not better & the line is hardly discernible, but in extreme cases several lines will be apparent & spoil the picture.

Cathode-Ray Tube

An electrical device for giving a visual indication of the magnitude, shape, etc., of an oscillating current. It may be also employed to provide actual images of wireless valve characteristics and/or other data. It consists of a large glass tube which is conical. The large end is coated on the inside with some fluorescent material.

At the point of the cone, or the narrow end of the tube, is sealed a cathode. A short distance from this cathode is fixed an anode. The arrangement so far, then, is a replica of an ordinary wireless valve, & it works on practically the same principles. If a negative on the base of the cone, one of the causes is the over-amplification of the higher frequencies.

III. MANUSCRIPT WORK   43

*cathode - part of the tube, in the form of a cylinder, & made of nickel.

‡anode : the positive pole of a voltaic current.

potential is applied to the ~~anode~~ cathode, or a positive potential applied to the anode, a stream of electrons will be shot off from the cathode, and will be driven w. great force on to the anode.

INSERT A

CAPS / stet. <u>focus coil</u> [a coil of wire through wh. a current passes through so to convert it into an electro-magnet. This is placed round the neck of the picture tube & brings the beam to focus at the tube face.

CAPS <u>Oscillatory Scanning</u> [both Name given to scanning methods by means of wh. the
trs light spot oscillates or travels backwards or forwards over the image to be televised. After ea. complete oscillation the light spot shifts laterally, thus enabling the new area of the picture to be scanned. Oscillatory scanning possesses many practical disadvantages.

INSERT B

CAPS <u>Raster</u> [RASTER]
The rectangular picture area built up by the scanning spot on the end of the cathode-ray tube.

CAPS <u>Synchronising Valve</u>
name given to the valve wh. in television circuits deals w. the synchronising currents.

CAPS <u>Video</u> [VIDEO]
T.V. term signifying picture or vision, as distinct from sound (audio).

a permanent magnet is often used in place of the electro-magnet.

(OVER

A **Contrast** — Term signifying the relationship between the degrees of shade & light in a picture, televised or otherwise.

B **Picture Frequency** — The number of complete images transmitted per second.

R.S.A.—ADVANCED 1971

CHAPTER IV

DISPLAYED WORK

1. General points about display. A typewritten document which is well displayed is pleasing to the eye, is easy to read, and makes it easy to see the most important parts. To be able to produce such work, the typist must be able to select the essential details, and to use her artistic ability effectively to arrange these within the whole. It is not always easy for a beginner, as experience plays a large part in acquiring this skill, but the basic requirements are that the document is neat, tidy and clean, simply arranged, and that the facts are clearly and effectively conveyed.

The following paragraphs describe some of the ways in which a document can be displayed, although it must be borne in mind that there is no right or wrong way to display anything, and what may be pleasing to one person may not suit another.

2. Headings. Main headings are centred over the line of writing, and are usually typed in either ordinary capitals, with one or two clear spaces between each word, or in spaced capitals, with three spaces between each word.

Sub-headings may be in capitals or in lower case, and can centred or typed at the left-hand margin. Sometimes shoulder headings are used, and these commence in the left-hand margin, two or three space to the left of the first margin stop.

3. Underscoring. Underscoring or underlining plays a very important part in an effective display, but it must be used with discretion. Important parts (especially in notices, announcements and similar documents), headings and sub-headings, may be underlined. Only one line should be typed—double underlining is never used in this type of work—and care must be taken to see that the line does not project beyond the first or last letter. Punctuation is never underlined, unless it occurs in the middle of the line.

4. Centring. In some types of displayed work (*e.g.* title pages, menus) it is necessary to centre every row horizontally, but it is not always necessary vertically to centre the whole. For example, the title of a book, which is the first item to be typed on a title page, looks better if it is typed slightly above the vertical mid-point, with the publisher's name near the bottom of the page. In other documents, such as reports, where there is considerable body to the text, only the headings, sub-headings, tabulated portions, etc., are centred.

5. Tabular statements. Statistical data and other similar information looks most effective when arranged as a table; if it is arranged properly it also makes it much easier to read and understand. When a table is necessary, its size must be calculated beforehand and the appropriate space allowed for it when arranging all the material on the page (*see* V).

6. Line-spacing. The amount of space left between the lines of typewriting makes a big difference to its overall appearance, especially in notices, title pages, and other work where all lines are centred on the page. To leave a large space above and below an item which is typed in ordinary or spaced capitals gives impact to that item, and it immediately stands out from the whole; an item in single-line spacing (whether in capital or small letters) is less prominent.

7. Ornamentation. Decorative borders or corner-pieces may be used on menus and concert programmes, but these must be kept as simple as possible, otherwise a great deal of time will be required for the typing. A printer has the facilities for elaborate ornamentation and a typist is not expected to produce work of that standard, but a simple border, such as that in Fig. 24, improves the appearance and does not take long to complete.

8. Some displayed documents. The following list shows some types of work where the appearance is greatly improved by effective display:

(*a*) *Title page of a book* (*see* Fig. 17). Here, the essential information required is:

(*i*) The title of the book.

(*ii*) The name of the author.
(*iii*) The name of the publisher.

```
        T H E    L I F E    O F    A N    E X I L E

                      AN   AUTOBIOGRAPHY

                             by

                       JOHN   J.   JOHNS




                           London
                      The Bead Press Ltd.
```

FIG. 17.—*A title page for a book*

These three items should be displayed prominently, and any additional wording (*e.g.* qualifications of the author) would be in small letters. Every row must be centred horizontally on the page.

(*b*) *List of Contents* (*See* Fig. 18). Here, several points are important.

(i) The heading "CONTENTS" is centred above the list, with two or three clear line-spaces between it and the first item.

```
                             CONTENTS


                                                            Page

          Preface  .   .   .   .   .   .   .   .   .   .     iii


          Chapter    I   .   .   .   .   .   .   .   .   .     1

          Chapter   II   .   .   .   .   .   .   .   .   .    20

          Chapter  III   .   .   .   .   .   .   .   .   .    42

          Chapter   IV   .   .   .   .   .   .   .   .   .    58

          Chapter    V   .   .   .   .   .   .   .   .   .    79

          Chapter   VI   .   .   .   .   .   .   .   .   .   102

          Chapter  VII   .   .   .   .   .   .   .   .   .   114

          Chapter VIII   .   .   .   .   .   .   .   .   .   131

          Chapter   IX   .   .   .   .   .   .   .   .   .   148

          Chapter    X   .   .   .   .   .   .   .   .   .   168
```

FIG. 18.—*A contents page for a book*

(ii) There must be equal margins of reasonable size, and the two columns (chapter headings and page numbers) are connected by leader dots (*see* V, **2** for rules regarding the typing of leader dots).

(iii) The complete list, with the heading, is centred vertically on the page.

(iv) If there are only a few items in the list, double-line spacing may be used, otherwise use single-line spacing.

(v) In the "page" column, the figures are typed directly underneath each other, *i.e.* units under units, tens under tens, etc.

(vi) If a chapter has been divided into sections (*see* Fig. 19), and the individual sections are to be listed, the word "CHAPTER" may be centred over the line of writing, or placed at the left-hand margin.

IV. DISPLAYED WORK

CONTENTS

		Page
Preface	. . . .	iii

AT HOME

Chapter	I	. . . .	1
Chapter	II	. . . .	20
Chapter	III	. . . .	42

AT SCHOOL

Chapter	IV	. . . .	58
Chapter	V	. . . .	79
Chapter	VI	. . . .	102
Chapter	VII	. . . .	114

AT WORK

Chapter	VIII	. . . .	131
Chapter	IX	. . . .	148
Chapter	X	. . . .	168

FIG. 19.—*A contents page for a book, showing section headings*

Well-qualified

S H O R T H A N D - T Y P I S T

required by

Managing Director of large Engineering Works.

Pleasant conditions.   Good salary.

Apply by letter to:

P.O. Box 14,
Newtown.

FIG. 20.—*A simple display for an advertisement*

BUSINESS TYPEWRITING

<u>J O H N S O N & B O W E N , L T D.</u>

will offer for SALE by PUBLIC AUCTION

(unless sold previously)

at

THE PROPERTY AUCTION ROOM
High Street, Newtown

on

THURSDAY, 14th MAY, 19--

at 7.30 p.m.

the property known as

<u>R O S E L E A   H O U S E</u>

BEAUFORT ROAD

NEWTOWN

An attractive detached double-fronted cottage on two
floors, in one acre of grounds.

Accommodation: hall, lounge, dining-room, breakfast-
room, kitchen, utility-room, four bedrooms, bathroom,
separate w.c., cellar, outside storage barn.

All main services

Freehold with vacant possession

Viewing and full particulars from

JOHNSON & BOWEN, LTD.
High Street,
Newtown.

FIG. 21.—*A displayed handbill*

IV. DISPLAYED WORK

R E E D   C O L T   &   C O   L T D.

APPLICATION FOR EMPLOYMENT

```
Name (in full)        ..........................................

Address               ..........................................

                      ..........................................

Date of birth ..................... Tel. No. ....................

Schools attended      ..........................................

                      ..........................................

                      ..........................................

Brief details of      ..........................................
any G.C.E. or C.S.E.
certificates held     ..........................................

                      ..........................................

Other qualifications  ..........................................

                      ..........................................

Type of employment    ..........................................
required
                      ..........................................

Details of relevant   ..........................................
experience
                      ..........................................

Names and addresses   ..........................................
of two referees
                      ..........................................

                      ..........................................

                      ..........................................


Signed ......................... Date ..........................
```

Fig. 22.—*An application form*

(c) *Advertisements, notices and handbills* (*see* Figs. 20 and 21). Documents such as these should be typed according to paragraphs **1–6** above.

(d) *Application forms* (*see* Fig. 22). The wording on the form (*e.g.* name, address, qualifications, etc.) should be displayed effectively, making sure that adequate dotted lines are included. It is not necessary to leave at least one whole line for every item, as some (*e.g.*, "tel. no.") require only a small space; others (*e.g.* "address") require more than one line of dots, and the number of line-spaces required

MR. and MRS. F. B. JONES

request the pleasure of the company of

....

at

AN INFORMAL DINNER PARTY

to be held at

THE RED LION HOTEL, CROOME

on

Saturday, 24th July, 19--

at 7.30 p.m. for 8 p.m.

R.S.V.P.

16 Burden Road,
Croome.

Fig. 23.—*An invitation*

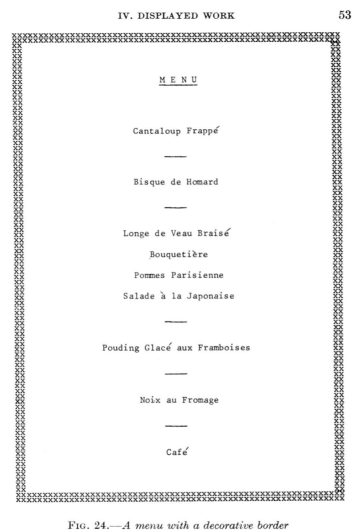

Fig. 24.—*A menu with a decorative border*

should be worked out carefully beforehand. The whole should be centred vertically and horizontally on the page, and the rules regarding the typing of dotted lines (II, **4**) should be carefully followed.

(*e*) *Invitations* (*see* Fig. 23). Several points should be remembered here.

   (*i*) Formal invitations may be typed on A5- or A6-size paper or card.
   (*ii*) Every row is centred across the page.
   (*iii*) The wording is always in the third person.
   (*iv*) The address of the sender (with R.S.V.P. typed above it) is placed in the bottom left-hand corner.
   (*v*) It is usual to type a dotted line where the name of the person invited is to appear; after the invitations are printed or duplicated, the individual names are inserted, so sufficient space must be left above the dotted line for this. If only a few invitations are required, each is typed individually and the name inserted at this stage.
   (*vi*) An acceptance of an invitation is typed in exactly the same manner as the invitation itself, but as each invited person has only one reply to send, there will never be any need to use dotted lines for the subsequent insertion of a name.
   (*vii*) Invitations may be decorated with a border if the subject of the invitation is suitable.

(*f*) *Menus* (*see* Fig. 24). Typed on any suitably sized card or paper, these give plenty of scope for attractive display, and ornamental borders or corner-pieces may be included. Each item on the menu is separated, and a larger space (often with a decorative dividing line) is left between the courses. The whole menu must be centred horizontally and vertically on the page. If the menu is in French, great care must be taken with the spelling, especially if the typist is unfamiliar with the language. Accents, etc., must be neatly inserted in black ink after the typing is completed.

PROGRESS TEST 4

1. Suggest how:

   (*a*) a main heading,
   (*b*) a sub-heading,

may be displayed most effectively. (**2–4**)

2. How does the intelligent use of line-spacing affect the appearance of displayed matter? (**6**)

3. When might a typist use ornamentation? (**7**)

4. Draw a rough diagram, showing how you would set out the

IV. DISPLAYED WORK

title page of a book, to include the title of the book, the name and qualifications of the author, and the name of the publisher. (**2–8**)

5. Draft an effectively displayed advertisement containing the following information:

For sale, portable typewriter in good condition, very little used, well-known make, £15 or near offer, telephone 04–444–3921 after 6 p.m. (**2–8**)

6. What are the generally accepted rules regarding the typing of formal invitations? (**8**)

7. How may a menu be well displayed? (**8**)

BUSINESS TYPEWRITING

On a sheet of plain white A4 paper, type one copy of the following in single-line spacing with double between paragraphs.

EDUCATION DEPARTMENT

MEMORANDUM TO ALL HEAD TEACHERS/COOK SUPERVISORS

Salaries and Wages Enquiries

The staff *of the Salaries + Wages Section* will be moving to new accommodation in "Manston House", on Wednesday, 19th August, 1970. and Thursday, 20th August, As it will be difficult to contact the staff on these days, would you please defer any queries until the Friday.

(a) The new telephone extension numbers are as follows:-

Section → *centre*	Extension
Teachers - Primary	362
Teachers - Secondary	360
Teachers - Further Education / All non-teaching staff paid monthly	361
All employees paid on claim	356
School caretakers and cleaners	352
School Meals Service - Primary	349
Secondary / Further Education	357

(b) Although there is a change of address, will you please continue to forward your time sheets in the green envelope until all my existing stock is exhausted.

P. B. STEVENS,

Education Officer

August, 1970

(Which is addressed to the Town Hall)

I set out below some information relative to their location + the new telephone extension numbers which will apply from that day.

R.S.A.—ELEMENTARY 1970

CHAPTER V

TABULATION

1. General points about tabular work. Tabulation is the setting out of information in the form of a table with two or more columns. The table can be of any size, and the columns, which may contain writing or figures, may or may not be enclosed by ruled lines. The general rules applying to all forms of tabular work are as follows:

(a) Use paper of any suitable size, but it must be measured very carefully before any calculations are made. The width is measured in terms of typewriting characters, and the depth is measured in terms of line-spaces. Both measurements are taken exactly from the edge of the paper. The two most common sizes of typewriting characters are:

(i) *Pica type:* ten characters per inch.
(ii) *Elite type:* twelve characters per inch.

There are other sizes, however, and individual typewriters should be checked with a ruler. With nearly all typewriters there are six line-spaces to the inch, regardless of the size of the actual typeface.

(b) Make a rough plan of the table on a spare piece of paper, marking in all measurements and calculations. Write in the number of characters in the individual columns, margin points, tabulator stop positions, allocation of line-spaces, and any other notes regarding the display, etc.

(c) All arithmetical calculations must be worked out, and checked carefully, before commencing to type.

(d) The complete table, including any headings and/or footnotes, must be centred vertically and horizontally on the page, *i.e.* with equal margins at either side, and an equal space above and below the table.

(e) Main headings and sub-headings above and in the table must be centred on the page unless special instructions are given.

(*f*) A heading above a column must be centred over that column.

(*g*) When inserting the paper in the machine, the paper must be lined up at point 0 on the typewriting scale. You should always type across the rows, making full use of the tabulator stop and not down each column in turn.

(*h*) Leader dots may be inserted after the "descriptive" column (*see* below).

(*i*) Footnotes below the table are centred on the page, and they are typed in the same manner as in other documents (*see* III, 7).

(*j*) Any ruling may be done by using the underscore key, or with pen and ink (or ball-point pen) afterwards; a combination of both is also acceptable but pencilled ruling is not allowed unless specially instructed.

2. Leader dots. Leader dots are meant to lead the eye from one column to the next, and are used when there is a fair amount of space between the columns. When typing leader dots, certain important points must be borne in mind:

(*a*) Leader dots may be typed as follows:

(*i*) In groups of two, with three spaces between the groups.
(*ii*) In groups of three, with two spaces between the groups.
(*iii*) As regularly spaced single dots.
(*iv*) As a continuous line of dots.

A continuous line of dots is not recommended if many have to be inserted, as this can distract from the main content of the table (*see* below).

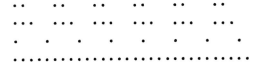

(*b*) Leader dots must always be typed lightly and evenly.

(*c*) At least one clear space must be left between the last letter or figure in one column, and the first dot; and one clear space between the last dot and the first figure or letter of the next column (or the ruled line).

V. TABULATION 59

(*d*) The groups of leader dots must be exactly underneath one another; use only one style of grouping in any one table.

(*e*) Each row of dots must finish at the same point, even though each row may commence at a different place.

(*f*) No line of writing or figures must go beyond the last dot in the rows above or below.

(*g*) The rows of writing or figures in the first column may be of different lengths and, as all groups of dots must be lined up underneath one another, there may be a varying number of clear spaces between the writing and the first dots. Each group of dots must always be complete, *e.g.* if groups of two are being used, there must never be a single dot at the beginning or end of a row. (*See* below.)

At least one clear space before first dot

Typewriting	..	..	..	4
Shorthand	..	..	..	32
Office Practice	..	..	..	78
Secretarial Duties	..	..	..	146

Dots all finish at same point

At least one clear space after last dot

3. Tables without ruling.

(*a*) Draw the plan on rough paper (*see* Fig. 25).

(*b*) Measure the exact width of the typing paper in terms of typewriter characters and note this on the rough paper.

(*c*) Count the number of characters and spaces in the longest row of each column—the longest rows may be in the column headings or in the general matter. Note these amounts on the rough plan.

(*d*) Add together these amounts (from (*c*)); this will give the total number of typewriting characters across the page.

(*e*) Subtract this total from the width of the paper measurement—this will give the total amount of clear spaces left across the page.

(*f*) These clear spaces must now be divided between the two margins and the gaps between the columns. Decide on suitable margins (which must be equal), and subtract these from the total amount of clear spaces. Note the margin widths on the rough plan.

(*g*) The remaining spaces are now divided amongst the

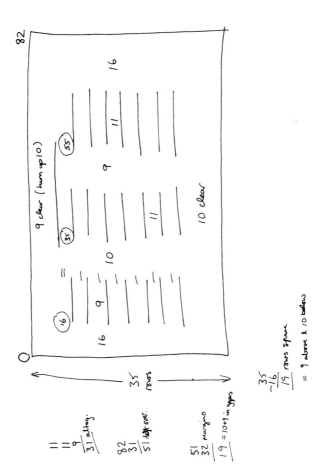

Fig. 25.—*Rough plan of a tabular statement without ruling, calculated for pica type on A5 paper*

Well-known Composers

Bach	Haydn	Schubert
Beethoven	Liszt	Schumann
Berlioz	Mozart	Sibelius
Brahms	Paganini	Tchaikovsky
Chopin	Puccini	Verdi
Elgar	Rachmaninov	Vivaldi
Handel	Rossini	Wagner

FIG. 26.—*A completed table*

gaps between the columns. If possible, the gaps should be the same size, but it is often necessary to insert odd "remainder" spaces in one or two of the gaps. If there is one space left over, insert this in the gap after the descriptive column (usually the first column). Note the widths of all gaps on the rough plan.

(*h*) If leader dots are required after the first (or any other) column, the gap after this column should be wider than after the other columns. This must be allowed for when dividing up the spaces (after having calculated the margins), and it should be so arranged that all the other gaps are if possible exactly equal.

(*i*) The margin and tabulator stops can now be worked out and noted on the rough plan. It is best to put a ring around all figures indicating a margin or tabulator stop, as there will then be no chance of the typist confusing these numbers with the other measurements noted down. Work out the tabulator stop numbers as follows:

    (*i*) Left-hand margin stop as decided in (*f*).

    (*ii*) Add together the margin stop, the number of characters in the longest row of the first column, and the number of spaces in the first gap. The total now arrived at gives the setting for the first tabulator stop.

    (*iii*) Add together the first tabulator stop number, the number of characters in the longest row of the second column, and the number of spaces in the second gap. The total now arrived at gives the setting for the second tabulator stop.

    (*iv*) Continue in this manner (*i.e.* adding together the previous tabulator stop number, the number of characters in the longest row of the column, and the following gap) until the last tabulator stop setting has been calculated.

    (*v*) To check that the calculations are correct, add together the last tabulator stop number, the number of characters in the longest row of the last column, and the spaces in the right-hand margin. The total now arrived at should equal the total number of spaces across the width of the typing paper.

(*j*) Measure the exact depth of the typing paper in terms of typewriting line-spaces, and note this on the rough plan.

(*k*) Count the total number of line-spaces in the table, including any headings, footnotes and clear line-spaces in between the writing.

V. TABULATION

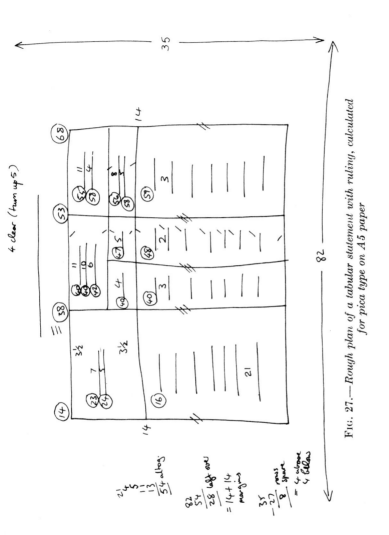

Fig. 27.—Rough plan of a tabular statement with ruling, calculated for pica type on A5 paper

(*l*) Subtract this last total from the total of (*j*); this will give the number of line-spaces to be left clear above and below the table.

(*m*) The number of clear line-spaces now arrived at must be divided by two; half for above the table, and half for below the table. If there is an odd number, put the extra line-space at the top. Note these numbers on the rough plan. The table is now ready for typing.

(*n*) Insert paper in the machine and set margin and tabulator stops as previously calculated and noted on the plan. Turn up the correct number of clear line-spaces and commence typing.

NOTE: The number of line-spaces turned up before commencement of typing must be one more than calculated, because the last of these will be filled up with the first row of typewriting, *e.g.* if ten clear-line spaces are required above the table, the typist must turn up eleven.

(*o*) When typing the table, the heading of a column, and the data in that column, will not necessarily both be typed at the tabulator stop position (unless both are the same length). If the heading was the longest row used for the calculations, then the longest row in the actual column is centred underneath this, and all other data in that column will commence at this point. If the heading was not the longest row, then it must be centred above the column.

4. Tables with ruling. Follow the instructions given in **3** for tables without ruling, up to and including point (*c*), *see* also Fig. 27. Then:

(*a*) Add together:

- (*i*) The amounts calculated for the longest row of each column.
- (*ii*) Two spaces for each of the outside vertical rulings (one space for each ruled line and one for a clear space before commencing or after completing typing in the columns).
- (*iii*) Three spaces each for all other vertical rulings (one space for a ruled line and a clear space either side of it).

The total now arrived at will give the total horizontal space necessary for the table, including all vertical ruled lines.

NOTE: If it is desired, and if the width of the paper permits, five spaces may be allowed for each inside vertical line instead of three, in which case three spaces each, instead of two, will be allowed for the outside vertical lines.

(*b*) Subtract this total from the width of the paper measurement—this will now give the amount of space left for the margins.

(*c*) Divide this last figure by two, and the answer gives the widths of the margins. If there is an odd space left over, this is usually added to the gap after the descriptive column, making one extra space there; margins will then be equal. Note the margin width on the rough plan.

(*d*) If the margins appear to be excessively wide, it may be necessary to reduce them equally, and add the extra spaces to the gap after the descriptive column; when typing, this gap can be filled in with leader dots.

(*e*) The margin and tabulator stops can now be worked out and noted on the rough plan. Do not set the first margin stop at the actual margin width, as the typing will commence two spaces further on (because one space is left clear after the outside ruled line). Set the margin and tabulator stops as follows:

(*i*) Margin stop at margin width, plus two.

(*ii*) Add together the number in (*i*) and the number of characters in the longest row of the first column (plus any extra spaces). Add three (for the ruled line plus one space either side) to this total. The sum now arrived at gives the tabulator stop for the commencement of typing in the second column.

(*iii*) Continue in this manner, *i.e.* adding together the previous tabulator stop number, the number of characters in the longest row of each column, plus a further three, until the last tabulator stop has been calculated.

(*iv*) To calculate the right-hand margin stop, add together previous tabulator stop, the number of characters in the last column, plus a further two. The total now arrived at gives the point on the scale for the outside ruled line at the right-hand side. Note this on the plan.

(*v*) To check that the calculations are correct, add together the number of the outside ruled line and the margin width. The total now arrived at should equal the total number of spaces across the width of the typing paper.

(f) The ruled lines are usually drawn in after all the typewriting in the table is completed, and when the paper is taken out of the machine. To assist with the ruling, it is best lightly to mark the position of the ruled lines with a stencil dot (*see* Fig. 28), placed where the ends of the lines will fall when actually typing the table. The positions of these stencil dots may be noted on the rough plan, and are calculated as follows:

Sizes of Paper

Sizes of paper	Typewriting characters across		Line spaces down
	Pica	Elite	Pica and Elite
A4	82½	99	70½
A5 (vertically)	59	71	50

Fig. 28.—*Placing the stencil dots before ruling*

(i) The first dot (for the left-hand vertical edge of the table), is at the position decided on for the width of the margins as in (c).

(ii) The second dot (for the first inside vertical ruled line), is at the first tabulator stop less two spaces; then one clear space will be left in between the typewriting and the line.

(iii) The third dot is at the second tabulator stop less two spaces; and so on, until all inside vertical line dots are complete.

(iv) The position for the last dot (for the right-hand vertical edge of the table) is arrived at by subtracting the margin width from the total width of the typing paper.

(g) Measure the exact depth of the typing paper in terms

of typewriting line-spaces, and note this on the rough plan.

(*h*) Count the total number of line-spaces in the table, making sure that at least one clear space is left on either side of any horizontal ruled line. The horizontal lines themselves *do not* take up any space and so do not get added into this total. Count all headings and footnotes.

(*i*) Subtract this last total from the total number of line-spaces in the paper; this will give the number of line-spaces to be left clear above and below the table.

(*j*) Divide this number by two; half for above the table and half for below the table. Note these numbers on the rough plan. The table is now ready for typing.

(*k*) Insert paper in the machine and set margins and tabulator stops as previously calculated. Consult the rough plan and the original copy all the time when typing the table, and insert the stencil dots where necessary. Great care must be taken to see that the platen is turned up the correct amount before and after stencilling the dots. If you

Sizes of Paper

Sizes of paper	Typewriting characters across		Line spaces down
	Pica	Elite	Pica and Elite
A4	$82\frac{1}{2}$	99	$70\frac{1}{2}$
A5 (vertically)	59	71	50
A5 (horizontally)	$82\frac{1}{2}$	99	35
Foolscap	80	96	78
Quarto	80	96	60
Octavo (vertically)	50	60	48
Octavo (horizontally)	80	96	30

FIG. 29.—*A completed table*

want to leave one clear space below a row of typing and above any stencilled dots, turn up once from the typing; to leave one clear space below the stencilled dots and above any typing, turn up twice from the dots (this is because a row of typewriting fills up one line-space, whereas a dot does not).

(*l*) When the typewriting is complete, rule the lines with pen and ink, or ball-point pen. When ruling remember the following points:

    (*i*) Use a clean, flat surface.
    (*ii*) Use a ruler that is long enough for the longest line.
    (*iii*) There must be no blobs of ink.
    (*iv*) The lines must not be too thick.
    (*v*) The lines must fit exactly between the stencil dots.
    (*vi*) The lines must join exactly at the corners, with a neat right-angle.
    (*vii*) Rule the outside frame before the inner lines.

(*m*) When typing large tables, it may not be possible to allow three clear spaces for each ruled line. In these cases, when calculating the tabulator stop positions, allow two spaces between each column, and one clear line-space where the horizontal lines are to be (*i.e.* turn up two between each block of typewriting). Dots are not stencilled, and the lines are ruled afterwards using personal judgment to decide their position; a clear plastic ruler makes it fairly easy to see when they are centrally placed.

(*n*) If, after allowing only two spaces between columns, the table is still too large for the width of the paper, shorten the width of the descriptive column by running the longest rows on into two rows each—this, of course, makes the table longer in depth. When using two or more rows for an item, the second row is indented one or two spaces.

5. Vertical headings. When the headings over the columns in a ruled table are rather long, and yet the data within the columns is short, it may be practicable to type those headings vertically, *i.e.* at right angles to, or at a slant to, the main direction of the typewriting. This frequently occurs with statistical tables containing monthly data, where the names of the months form the column headings (*see* Fig. 30).

When typing a table with vertical headings, the appropriate amount of space required for the headings is left clear and they are inserted after all other typewriting is completed. To

	January	February	March	April	May	June
Great Britain	16	21	32	40	79	80
France	10	60	62	79	79	84
Spain	14	94	91	80	82	81

FIG. 30.—*Part of a tabular statement, showing vertical headings*

calculate the required amount of space for the vertical headings:

(a) It is necessary to know how many typewriting characters equal 1 in., and how many line-spaces equal 1 in.

As we have seen, the number of typewriting characters varies with the size of the type, but the usual amounts are ten per inch in pica type and twelve per inch in élite type. The number of line-spaces is six per inch, regardless of the size of type.

(b) Prepare a rough plan, with the vertical headings marked in. Then count the number of characters in the longest row of the vertical headings, and add two to this amount—this is to allow one clear space above and below the heading. Note this total on the rough plan.

(c) The total in (b) is now converted into inches, which in turn, are converted into line-spaces. The calculations are worked out in the following manner:

Assume the number of characters (plus two) in the vertical heading is fourteen, and the type is pica (ten characters per inch), then:

$$\frac{14}{10} = 1\tfrac{2}{5} \text{ in.}$$

$$1\tfrac{2}{5} \times 6 = \frac{7}{5} \times 6 = \frac{42}{5} = 8\tfrac{2}{5} \text{ line-spaces.}$$

Therefore, 8½ line-spaces would be allowed for that particular vertical heading.

The table below shows some examples already worked out:

		No. of characters (plus two) in vertical heading	10	12	14	15	17	20	21	24
Pica Type	{	Measurement (in.)	1	$1\frac{1}{5}$	$1\frac{2}{5}$	$1\frac{1}{2}$	$1\frac{7}{10}$	2	$2\frac{1}{10}$	$2\frac{2}{5}$
		(mm)	25	30	35	37	42.5	50	52.5	60
		Line-spaces	6	7	$8\frac{1}{2}$	9	10	12	$12\frac{1}{2}$	$14\frac{1}{2}$
Elite type	{	Measurement (in.)	$\frac{5}{6}$	1	$1\frac{1}{6}$	$1\frac{1}{4}$	$1\frac{5}{12}$	$1\frac{2}{3}$	$1\frac{3}{4}$	2
		(mm)	20	25	29	31	35	41	44	50
		Line-spaces	5	6	7	$7\frac{1}{2}$	$8\frac{1}{2}$	10	$10\frac{1}{2}$	12

(d) The number of line-spaces now calculated is noted on the rough plan, and this is the amount of space to be left clear between the horizontal ruled lines for the vertical headings to be inserted later.

(e) The width required for each "box" for the vertical headings depends on whether the width of the column underneath is wider or narrower than the heading itself. If the column is wider, the column is the amount that must be allowed for, and, in order to get the headings properly centred, the complete width (from ruled line to ruled line) must be converted into line-spaces when typing the vertical headings. If the column is narrower than the vertical heading, the line-spaces required for the heading are converted back into character spaces, and these are allowed for in the width of the column. In the latter case, the column data is centred within the width of that column.

(f) The rest of the table is planned in the normal way, as described in 3. If horizontal headings appear with the vertical headings, they must be centred in the appropriate box.

(g) After completing all typewriting except the vertical headings, remove the paper from the machine and rule the lines. Re-insert the paper in the correct position for the typing of the vertical headings, *i.e.* the left-hand margin of the table will now be at the top of the paper.

(h) Using the paper release lever, position the ruled

horizontal line (now vertical), which will be immediately below the completed vertical headings, at any exact point on the typewriting scale. Set the margin one point further on —this will allow one clear space either side of the heading.

(*i*) Using the variable line-spacer and the alignment scale, roll the platen into such a position that the vertical line (now horizontal) which will be to the left of the completed vertical heading, is lined up at the point of typewriting. Turn up the appropriate amount for typing the heading, *i.e.* centring the heading within the box.

EXAMPLES:

If the width of the box has been calculated as five line-spaces (*see* (*e*)), and the vertical heading consists of one row of typewriting, the typist would turn up three from the ruled line, and then type. This would allow two clear line-spaces above and below the heading.

If the width of the box has been calculated as five line-spaces, and the vertical heading consists of two lines of typewriting, the typist would turn up two-and-a-half from the ruled line, and then type. This allows one-and-a-half clear line-spaces above and below the heading.

(*j*) Each vertical heading must be positioned individually, and this involves the use of the variable line-spacer and the alignment scale every time, in order to position each heading correctly, as described in (*h*) and (*i*).

PROGRESS TEST 5

1. How many typewriting characters are there per inch with:
   (*a*) Pica type.
   (*b*) Elite type? (**1**)
2. How many line-spaces are there per inch with:
   (*a*) Pica type.
   (*b*) Elite type? (**1**)
3. Give three different ways of grouping leader dots. (**2**)
4. What points must be borne in mind when typing leader dots? (**2**)
5. The lines in tables are often ruled in red ink—what must be remembered when ruling these lines? (**4**)
6. How would you fit a very large tabulation on to the page when it is not possible to allow three clear spaces for each vertical ruled line? (**4**)
7. Describe how you would calculate the space required for a vertical heading. (**5**)

BUSINESS TYPEWRITING

Type a copy of the following price list.

trs/

MATERIALS FOR YATCH REPAIRS

	½ gallon	¼ gallon	1 pint
	£	£	£
ENAMELS			
White and Black	2.50	1.37½	0.75
Dark Grey and Dark Blue	–	1.37½	0.75
All other shades*	2.60	1.42½	0.77½
UNDERCOATS			
White and Black	2.17½	1.22½	0.67½
All other shades*	2.27½	1.27½	0.70
COLOURED POLYURETHANE	–	1.82½	0.99
VARNISH	1.75	0.95	0.55
THINNERS			
For Polyurethane	–	0.62½	0.35
For PVC Coating	–	0.65	0.36
PRIMERS			
Pink Priming**	1.90	1.00	0.55
Metallic Pink Priming	1.80	0.95	0.52½
Glassfibre Primer	1.95	1.05	0.62½

* Colour charts will be sent on request.

** Also available in 1-gallon tins.

Note to Typist – Please type lower-case words in 'hanging' form under the side headings – as example below.

ENAMELS

    White and Black
    Dark Grey, etc.

UNDERCOATS

    White and Black
    etc.

R.S.A.—ELEMENTARY 1970

V. TABULATION

Type one copy of the following on plain white paper. No ruling is required but you must underscore the underlined words and figures.

EXCELSIOR INSURANCE COMPANY

Premiums will be quoted after an application form has been completed.

TREBLE LINE SPACE HERE

TABLE A →

RUN ON

The limit of your liability

Caps.

	DRIVER'S AGE			
	17-21	22-26	27-32	OVER 32 l.c.
Policy holder, or wife/husband of policyholder driving	£40	£30	£20	£15
Sons or daughters driving	£55	£40	£20	£15
Others driving	£100	£60	£33	£20

TREBLE LINE SPACE HERE

TABLE B →

RUN ON

Liability for Sports Cars

Caps.

	DRIVER'S AGE			
	17-22	23-28	29-32	OVER 32 l.c.
Policyholder, or wife/husband, or son or daughter	£150	£100	£40	£15
Others driving	£200	£140	£60	£25
	(3)	(2)	(1)	

TREBLE LINE SPACE HERE

TRS./ NOTE: ←The Road Vehicles [Licensing] and] Registration] Regulations, 1964, require that whoever is registered as the owner shall be the person by whom the vehicle is kept and used. A valid policy cannot, therefore, be issued in the name of a parent if the main user of son or \ the car is in fact the \ daughter.

R.S.A.—ADVANCED 1970

Type one copy of the table and rule up. Please re-arrange the information so that the periods of repayments are used as column headings as follows:—

Amount of Loan	Monthly Repayments over:				
	12 months	24 months	36 mths.	48 mths.	60 mths.
£	£	£	£	£	£
500	43.75	22.91	15.97	12.50	10.41
400	35.00				

etc.   etc.

Please rule, or type, a horizontal line between the figures for loans of £100 and £90.

Caps: Repayment Tables for Loans

Monthly Repayments for Loans of:

Period of Repayment	£500	£400	£300	£200	£100	£90	£80	£70	£60	£50	£40	£30	£20	£10
12 months	43.75	35.00	26.25	17.50	8.75	7.87	7.00	6.12	5.25	4.37	3.50	2.62	1.75	0.87
24 months	22.91	18.33	13.75	9.16	4.58	4.12	3.66	3.21	2.75	2.29	1.83	1.37	0.91	0.46
36 months	15.97	12.78	9.58	6.39	3.19	2.87	2.55	2.24	1.91	1.54	1.28	0.96	0.64	0.32
48 "	12.50	10.00	7.50	5.00	2.50	2.25	2.00	1.75	1.50	1.25	1.00	0.75	0.50	0.25
60 "	10.41	8.33	6.25	4.19	2.08	1.87	1.66	1.46	1.25	1.04	0.88	0.62	0.41	0.21

The right is reserved to make alteration without notice.

CHAPTER VI

COMMERCIAL DOCUMENTS

1. A typical business transaction. The number and type of documents used for a business transaction varies a great deal, according to the nature of the business carried on, and also, to some extent, to the managerial requirements of any particular firm. Every firm, though, whether large or small, is required by law to keep accurate records of its financial state, and this means that some documents (*e.g.* invoices) are common to all types of business, and they all contain the same (or very similar) information, although that information may be presented in many different ways.

Because of these varied methods of presentation, this chapter can describe only typical layouts, and give general hints about the information to be typed on any particular document. There can be no standard layout, because business firms follow their own preferences, but the typist should always try to set out the information in a clear and uncluttered manner, making it as easy to read and understand as possible. Great care must be taken to present the facts accurately, with all reference numbers, order numbers, dates and sums of money, clearly stated in a prominent position.

A typical business transaction could be as follows:

(*a*) Enquiry.
(*b*) Quotation.
(*c*) Order.
(*d*) Delivery of goods.
(*e*) Invoice.
(*f*) Statement.
(*g*) Payment.

Several of the documents necessary in a business transaction contain almost identical information, and it is usual nowadays for all these to be typed simultaneously on a typewriter with continuous-stationery attachments, or special computerised

ENQUIRY   No. 6742

THE WOOL SHOP

Compton Town, GL5 19B

Date 2nd August, 19--

To: The Wool Mills,
     Beaverton,
     Lancs.

We would be pleased if you could supply a quotation for the goods listed below:

Quantity	Description
6 doz.	1 oz Balls double-knitting wool - pale blue.
6 doz.	1 oz Balls double-knitting wool - dark blue.
3 doz.	1 oz Balls 4-ply knitting wool - white.

For delivery not later than October, 19--

for THE WOOL SHOP

....

FIG. 31.—*A completed enquiry form*

equipment. All the forms would be together in a roll, with a carbon coating on the backs of the forms at the appropriate places. Forms that could be typed together include the advice note, delivery note, invoice, and copies for the various departments.

VI. COMMERCIAL DOCUMENTS

2. Enquiry. When a written enquiry is sent to a firm, it can take the form of an ordinary business letter, perhaps asking for a catalogue or price list, or requesting a quotation for specific

```
                    JOHN BROWN & CO. LTD.
                         High Street,
                            Bristol.

                                    Date as postmark

    Dear Sir,

    We acknowledge receipt of your enquiry which is
    receiving our best attention.

                            Yours faithfully,

                         JOHN BROWN & CO. LTD.
```

FIG. 32.—*A typical reply card*

goods or services. If a quotation is required, it is important that the following details are included in the letter of enquiry:

(a) Description of required goods (with catalogue number, if available).

(b) Quantity and quality of goods.

(c) Size (if applicable).

(d) Required date of delivery.

(e) Request for information on discounts, transport, etc.

The enquiry may also be on an official printed form (*see* Fig. 31).

When the letter of enquiry is received by the seller, it should receive prompt attention, and if it is not possible to send out the necessary details immediately, a ready-printed card (*see* Fig. 32) could be sent informing the prospective buyer that his enquiry is receiving attention.

3. Quotation, estimate and tender. A *quotation* is the name given to a document which quotes prices and descriptions of the goods, discounts available, delivery dates and transport arrangements   An *estimate* is similar to a quotation and is, in fact, the supplier's quotation for carrying out some work

<u>QUOTATION</u>   No. 15870

T H E   W O O L   M I L L S

BEAVERTON

Lancs.

Enquiry No. 6742   4th August, 19--

The Buyer,
The Wool Shop,
Compton Town, GL5 19B

Quantity	Description	Price
6 doz.	1 oz Balls double-knitting wool - pale blue.	9p/ball
6 doz.	1 oz Balls double-knitting wool - dark blue.	9p/ball
3 doz.	1 oz Balls 4-ply knitting wool - white.	10p/ball
	For acceptance within 21 days. Terms: 20% trade discount. $2\frac{1}{2}$% monthly account. Delivery: B.R.S. carriage paid.	

FIG. 33.—*A quotation*

according to specific instructions, *e.g.* plumbing, house repairs; an estimate may also be given for a service instead of for actual goods, *e.g.* hotel facilities for a conference. A *tender* is the same as an estimate, but the term is used when the work or service to be undertaken is for a local authority or other public body.

ORDER   No. 6400

THE WOOL SHOP

Compton Town, GL5 19B

Your quotation No. 15870   7th August, 19--

To: The Wool Mills,
    Beaverton,
    Lancs.

Please supply:

Quantity	Description	Price
6 doz.	1 oz Balls double-knitting wool - pale blue.	9p/ball
6 doz.	1 oz Balls double-knitting wool - dark blue.	9p/ball
3 doz.	1 oz Balls 4-ply knitting wool - white.	10p/ball

Terms and delivery as quoted.

FIG. 34.—*An order form*

A quotation may take the form of a normal business letter, but more commonly it is typed on a special quotation form (*see* Fig. 33).

4. Order. If the quotation is satisfactory to the buyer, an order will follow, and this must be typed on the firm's official printed order form (*see* Fig. 34). The order forms are numbered, and several carbon copies will be required for the various departments, *e.g.* for stores or accounts. Exact details regarding quantity and quality of the goods (with the reference number of the seller's quotation), the terms and delivery information, must all be stated clearly.

5. Delivery of goods and advice note. The goods may be delivered to the buyer without any more exchange of documents, but it is quite usual to acknowledge the order by sending a reply card, similar to that shown in Fig. 32.

Some firms prefer a more formal acknowledgment, and this may take the form of a printed sheet setting out all the details, terms, etc. This is not usually sent if a full quotation has already been rendered, but it might be used if the buyer has, perhaps, ordered straight from a catalogue or price list without any previous correspondence with the seller.

In addition, especially if the buyer has had to wait some time for delivery, an *advice note* may be sent stating that the

```
                    JOHN BROWN & CO. LTD.,

                       17 High Street,
                          Bristol.

                              Date as postmark

        We are pleased to advise you that your goods
        have been despatched by rail on 8th July 19--.


                         JOHN BROWN & CO. LTD.
```

Fig. 35.—*An advice note*

goods have been despatched. This note may be only a printed postcard (*see* Fig. 35).

More often, the advice note is an exact copy of the delivery note (*see* below); but whatever its form, the advice note would be sent by post while the goods would be sent separately, perhaps by rail or road.

6. Delivery and receipt note. The goods are sent accompanied by a *delivery note* (*see* Fig. 36). This is to enable the

DELIVERY NOTE   No. 59316

THE WOOL MILLS

BEAVERTON

Lancs.

Order No. 6400   12th August, 19--

The Wool Shop,
Compton Town. GL5 19B

Please receive:

Quantity	Description	
6 doz.	1 oz Balls double-knitting wool - pale blue.	2 parcels
6 doz.	1 oz Balls double-knitting wool - dark blue.	2 parcels
3 doz.	1 oz Balls 4-ply knitting wool - white.	1 parcel
	Delivery: B.R.S.	

Fig. 36.—*A delivery note*

buyer to check the consignment on arrival. The information contained on this form is similar to that on the original order form, except that all prices, discounts, etc., are omitted. An exact copy of the delivery note may be used as a *receipt note*; this has to be signed by the customer on receiving the goods, and it will be returned to the seller, who will then know that the goods have been delivered.

7. Invoice. The invoice (*see* Fig. 37) is the bill for the goods

INVOICE   No. 43211

THE WOOL MILLS

BEAVERTON

Lancs.

Your order No. 6400   17th August, 19--

To: The Wool Shop,
     Compton Town, GL5 19B

Quantity	Description	Rate	Amount due
			£
6 doz.	1 oz Balls double-knitting wool - pale blue.	9p	6.48
6 doz.	1 oz Balls double-knitting wool - dark blue.	9p	6.48
3 doz.	1 oz Balls 4-ply knitting wool - white.	10p	3.60
			16.56
	Less trade discount 20%		3.31
	Total		£13.25

Fig. 37.—*An invoice*

or services received, and is usually sent after the delivery. The information is identical with that of the delivery note, but includes the amount due, shown in the right-hand column.

8. Credit and debit note. A *credit note* (*see* Fig. 38) is sent to a buyer when he is owed money by a seller. This may occur if the buyer returns chargeable "empties" (*i.e.* bottles or crates in which the goods were delivered and for which a charge was made, the amount being refundable when the bottles, etc., are returned); or if a mistake has been made on the invoice, with the buyer being overcharged; or if goods have been returned for some reason. Credit notes are always typed in red.

A *debit note* (*see* Fig. 39) is a note sent to a buyer when a mistake has been made on an invoice and he owes money to a seller. This note is typed in black.

CREDIT NOTE   No. 642

T H E   W O O L   M I L L S

BEAVERTON

Lancs.

To: Jones & Co. Ltd.,
    49 High Street,
    Lowtown.   19th August, 19--

| 24 | Towels - wrong colour | |
| | Returned 18th August, 19-- | £28.00 |

FIG. 38.—*A credit note (printed and typed in red)*

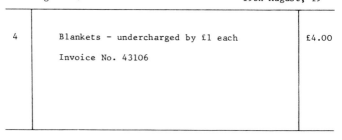

Fig. 39.—*A debit note (printed and typed in black)*

9. Statement and payment. A *statement of account* (*see* Fig. 40) is usually sent monthly to a buyer who has been allowed credit facilities by a seller. This means that the customer does not settle each invoice as it arrives, but waits for a statement which lists the invoices of all goods bought, with appropriate deductions or additions for discounts, credit notes, debit notes, etc. It also shows the amount of money owing at the beginning of the month, and deducts any cash which has been received since the previous statement was prepared; the final total is the balance due, which is usually settled with a cheque.

10. Commercial abbreviations. There are some abbreviations which are frequently used in commercial documents, and these need not necessarily be rendered in full: when typing them, the typist must follow the method generally practised by her own particular firm. A list of the most common abbreviations appears in Appendix I.

STATEMENT

THE WOOL MILLS

BEAVERTON

Lancs.

To: The Wool Shop,
Compton Town.
GL5 19B

Date	Particulars	Debit	Credit	Balance
19--		£	£	£
	Balance outstanding			9.30
2nd August	Invoice No. 42802	15.06		
4th August	Cheque	·	9.30	
17th August	Invoice No. 43211	13.25		
		28.31		
	Discount $2\frac{1}{2}$%		0.71	
			10.01	
				£27.60
				The last figure in this column is the amount due

Fig. 40.—*A statement*

PROGRESS TEST 6

1. Name six different commercial documents used in a general business transaction. Why is there no standard layout for the typing of these documents? (**1**)

2. What details, besides the appropriate names and addresses, should appear in a letter of enquiry? (**2**)

3. What is (*a*) a quotation, and (*b*) a tender? (**3**)

4. What information is included on the delivery note? How does this differ from that on the order form? (**6**)

5. Why are credit notes issued? Describe how they are typed. (**8**)

6. A statement of account is sent to the buyer at regular intervals. What information should the statement contain? (**9**)

VI. COMMERCIAL DOCUMENTS

Please type a copy of this letter on plain A4 paper. No date is required and no carbon copy.

Dear Sir / Madam,

We are pleased (glad) to send you a copy of our latest Garden Seed Catalogue which we hope you will find interesting. As a keen gardener, we look forward to the opportunity of supplying your seed requirements for next season.

Although we have long been known as specialists in new and unusual vegetable seeds, we also offer a comprehensive range of general garden seeds. All the varieties we offer have been tried and tested by our own experts + you can rely upon them being the v. best strains obtainable.

May we also draw your attention to our Garden Book which offers Roses, Flowering Trees + Shrubs + Fruit Trees. In this book you will find many plants + shrubs suitable for spring planting. If you have not received a copy we shall be very happy indeed to send you one.

We believe that our stocks of vegetable + flower seeds are the finest obtainable + our method of packing ensures that they reach you in peak condition to give first-class germination + strong plants. We have every confidence in our seeds + are sure that you will be v. pleased if you sow them.

We hope we may be favoured with your orders which will receive prompt + efficient attention.

Yours faithfully,

CHAPTER VII

LITERARY WORK

1. General points about literary work. In its broadest sense, literary work can include any typewritten material, sometimes intended for the printer. This section, however, deals with authors' manuscripts of books, essays, lectures, etc., unless otherwise stated.

The following rules apply to general literary work:

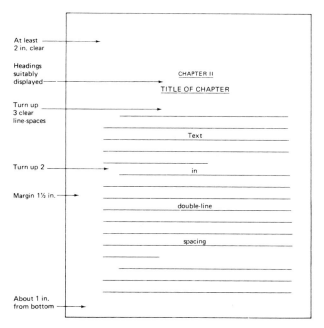

FIG. 41.—*Layout of the first page of a chapter*

(a) Use A4-size paper, and type on one side only.

(b) The final copy of the main text is typed in double-line spacing, with single-line spacing for quotations, extracts and footnotes. This is called a *fair copy*. A fair copy intended for the printer is typed wholly in double-spacing.

If the document is likely to be heavily corrected by the author, then the first typing could be in treble-line spacing—this leaves plenty of room for the corrections to be inserted. At this stage, the document is called a *draft copy*.

(c) There is a margin of approximately $1\frac{1}{2}$in. at the left-hand side (this may be wider for the draft copy), and approximately 1 in. at the right-hand side.

(d) Chapters are headed with the chapter numbers in large roman numerals and are typed about 2 in. from the top of the paper—this is called a *dropped heading*, and it occurs on the first page of every chapter (*see* Fig. 41). The heading is typed two or three line-spaces underneath the chapter number, and it is centred above the line of typing. All headings must be neatly displayed in block or spaced capitals.

(e) All pages except the first are numbered in arabic figures, which are centred at the top of the page, or, if the manuscript is intended for the printer, typed at the top right-hand side. The number is placed 1 in. from the top of the paper, and one or two line-spaces are left clear between the number and the continuation of the text. One inch is left clear at the foot of the page.

The pages of a book should be numbered consecutively throughout the text, *i.e.* the numbers should run continuously, regardless of where chapters begin or end.

(f) The preface or introduction of a book is numbered separately, in small roman numerals.

(g) A new sheet of paper is used for the beginning of each chapter, even if the last page of the previous chapter has only a few lines typed on it. The final page of a chapter which is not completely filled with writing is called a *short page*.

(h) A *tail-piece* may be required at the end of a chapter or section. This is a block of ornamental typing devised by the typist or the author, which fills up some of the space left on that page. It is centred under the line of writing and placed at least 1 in. below the last row of typewriting. A simple tail-piece is illustrated below, and another is shown in Fig. 42.

$$-\text{ooOoo}-$$
$$\text{ooo}$$
$$\text{o}$$

(*i*) When preparing a book, it is necessary to type separate pages for the title, the list of contents, and for the list of illustrations, and these should all be displayed effectively (*see* IV).

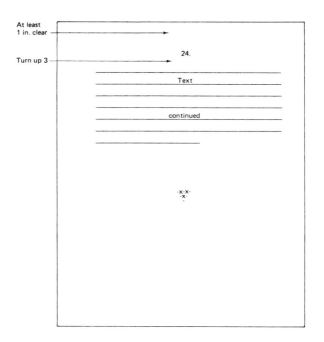

FIG. 42.—*Layout of the final page of a chapter, with a tail-piece*

(*j*) The general rules regarding the typing of manuscripts (*see* III) should be followed where applicable; special care should be taken regarding the positioning of any footnotes (*see* Figs. 15 and 16).

VII. LITERARY WORK

2. Quotation marks. Quotations and extracts may require quotation marks, in which case the following points should be noted:

(*a*) The author may decide to use either single or double quotation marks.

(*b*) When quoting prose, insert quotation marks at the beginning of each paragraph and at the end of the last paragraph (*i.e.* not at the end of every paragraph).

(*c*) When quoting poetry, insert quotation marks at the beginning of the first verse and at the end of the last verse.

(*d*) Quotations within a quotation should have single quotation marks if double marks are used at the beginning of the passage, or double quotation marks if single marks are used at the beginning of the passage.

(*e*) Quotation marks are generally placed outside the full stop and comma, although individual authors may have a style of their own. Other punctuation marks (in relation to the quotation marks) are positioned according to the sense of the passage, *i.e.* if the punctuation marks are part of the quotation, they are placed inside the quotation marks, otherwise they are placed outside them.

3. Estimating the length of a document. The typist should be able to estimate the approximate number of words per page of typewriting. The simplest way is to type a few lines of general matter, then the average number of words per line can be worked out. The number of lines per page varies with the size of the paper, but with A4-size paper and using double-line spacing (with margins of 1 in. at the top and bottom of the page) about 30 lines of typewriting can be accommodated on a page.

It is especially important to know how much can be typed on one page when there are several typists working on the same document. It is essential that the whole, when completed, should form a continuous *fit*—this means that each complete page fits in with those before and after it.

It is also important that all the typists use the same style of typewriter, and that margins, spacings, headings, method of numbering, etc. are uniform throughout.

4. Printer's proofs. It may sometimes be necessary for the typist or secretary to read through the printer's proofs, and if any corrections are necessary these must be marked with the appropriate printer's correction signs. A printer's proof marked with errors is called a *foul proof*.

Most of the correction signs are the same as the typists' correction signs (*see* III), although a few look the same but have different meanings, and some are used only by the printer.

(*a*) Correction signs which have a *different meaning for the typist and the printer* include the following:

- (*i*) *Words single-underlined.* To a typist this means "underline the words," but to a printer this means "use italic letters."
- (*ii*) *Words double-underlined.* To a typist this means "use capitals," but to a printer this means "use small capitals." It must be remembered that a printer has access to various sizes of type.
- (*iii*) *Words treble-underlined.* To a typist this means "use spaced capitals," but to a printer this means "use capitals."

(*b*) Correction signs which are used *only by the printer* include those shown on p. 93.

5. Plays. A complete play may be divided into the following sections:

(*a*) *Title page* (*see* Fig. 43). This forms the first page, and must be displayed effectively, making full use of capitals, spaced capitals, line spacings, etc., as described in IV. The information on this page includes the name of the play, the type of play (*e.g.* comedy, farce), the number of Acts, and the author's name.

(*b*) *Acts and scenery* (*see* Fig. 44). The synopsis of Acts and scenery forms the second page, and this, too, is displayed. The word "ACT" is typed in capitals, and large Roman numerals are used for the numbering of the Acts.

(*c*) *Characters and cast* (*see* Fig. 45). The characters and cast are listed on the third page, using leader dots to connect the names of the characters (on the left-hand side of the page) with these of the cast (on the right-hand side of the page). The list of characters is underlined, if it is written in lower case, otherwise it is typed in capitals, with no underlining.

(*d*) *List of costumes* (*see* Fig. 45). This may be typed on

Printers' Correction Signs

Correction sign		Meaning	Interpretation
In margin	In text		
ital.	Word(s) underlined once	Italics	Change to italic letter(s).
s.c.	Word(s) underlined twice	Small capitals	Change to small capitals.
Caps	Word(s) underlined three times	Capitals	Change to capital letter(s).
rom.	Word(s) circled	roman	Change to roman type.
×	Letter(s) circled	Damaged letter	Substitute good letter(s).
w.f.	Letter(s) circled	Wrong fount (fount is the style of type)	Change to correct letter(s).
↻	Letter(s) circled	Letter(s) upside down	Put letter(s) the correct way up.
=	=		Straighten line(s).
↑	↑		Raise line(s).
↓	↓		Lower line(s).
eq #	(between words) ∧	Equal space	Equalise spacing between words.
l	Space circled		Push down space.

a separate page, but if the list is short it might be included on the third page. The names of the characters are typed in a column on the left-hand side, and a description of their costumes on the right-hand side.

(e) *Text of the play.* The last section is the play itself, the typing of which is described in **6** below.

6. Typing the play.

(a) Use A4-size paper and type on one side only in single-line spacing; double-line spacing should be used to separate the speeches.

```
         T H E    P I C K - P O C K E T S




              A COMEDY IN THREE ACTS




                       by




                  H. R. FELLOWS
```

FIG. 43.—*The title page of a play*

(*b*) The first page (*see* Fig. 46) will have a dropped heading which can be displayed in spaced capitals; subsequent pages are numbered as for general literary work.

(*c*) The Act number is always typed in capital roman numerals, and the Scene number in small roman numerals.

(*d*) The names of the characters are typed in capitals in the left-hand margin, so the margin must be sufficiently wide to accommodate the longest name, plus 1in. — 1½in. clear margin at the extreme left. At least three spaces are left clear after the end of the longest name and before the main text. A margin of approximately 1in. is left at the right-hand side of the paper.

```
                    ACT   I

            At the house of Mr. Green


                      - - -


                    ACT   II

         A spring day in the local market


                      - - -


                   ACT   III

         That evening at the police station
```

FIG. 44.—*A synopsis of Acts*

(*e*) All parts not actually spoken (this includes descriptions of scenes, stage directions and names of characters) are either typed in red, or underlined in pen and red ink (or ball-point pen) after completion of the typing.

(*f*) The description of the scene, (at the beginning of each Scene) commences with the word "SCENE," typed in block capitals. It may be in block paragraph or hanging paragraph form (second and subsequent rows indented two or three spaces), but the modern practice is to type all paragraphs of the play, including the speeches, in block form.

(*g*) If stage directions consist of one or two words only and are included in a speech, they are typed, in brackets, along with the speech.

If the stage directions are more lengthy, they are typed separately and may be in block paragraph or hanging paragraph form.

Stage directions of less than one line in length, but not

CHARACTERS AND CAST

Bill	Julian Brown
Mick	Michael Derry
Tommy	Clement Andover
Mr. Green	John Sellinger
Julia Green	Margot Delbraith
Maid	Margaret Sloane
Lady Cranbourne	Jill Madison
Women in the market	Beryl Slater Phyl Johns
Chief Inspector	Martin Delbraith
Police Constable	John Phillips

COSTUMES

Bill) Mick) Tommy)	Rough, outdoor clothes; peaked caps and dirty boots.
Mr. Green	Dark lounge suit with white shirt and "old school" tie.
Julia Green	Smart light-weight suit and blouse. Matching shoes.
Maid	Maid's uniform.
Lady Cranbourne	Old-fashioned black lace dress. Black shoes. Elaborate coiffure. Much jewellery.
Women in the market	Everyday working clothes.
Chief Inspector) Police Constable)	Police uniforms.

FIG. 45.—*Characters and cast, with list of costumes*

VII. LITERARY WORK

THE PICK-POCKETS

ACT I

SCENE   The sitting-room of Mr. Green's house. Large sofa at centre, with several coffee-tables placed nearby; on one is a bottle of sherry. Doors at left and right with a window at back. Small table against left wall, covered with papers and writing materials. Framed portrait of Mr. Green hangs on wall above table.

(Enter left Mr. Green, followed by Bill, Mick and Tommy, still wearing their caps)

Mr. Green   Take a seat, my dear fellows, and explain to me exactly what your problem is.

(Bill, Mick and Tommy sit awkwardly on the sofa)

Mick   (In a broad Irish accent) Well, Sir, it's like this ....

Bill   (Interrupting) Let me explain, my English's better ....

Tommy   You're just as bad. None of you ever went to school.

Bill   Stop being rude to your pals. (Sees the sherry) Gosh! I would like a drink.

Mr. Green   Oh! I'm sorry. Would you care for a sherry?

(Nods from Bill, Mick and Tommy)

I'll just go and get some clean glasses.

(Exit Mr. Green left. Immediately Bill and Tommy make a grab for the sherry bottle. Mick stops them)

Mick   There's no need to steal it – he's offered us some, hasn't he? Perhaps we ought to take off our caps to drink it. (Looking around the room) I bet there's some valuable stuff in this house. Look out, here he comes.

(Enter Mr. Green with four glasses. He goes to a coffee-table and begins to pour the sherry)

FIG. 46.—*The first page of a play (underscoring typed in red)*

included in a speech, may be centred over the line of writing, and bracketed.

7. Actors' parts. Actors' parts (see Fig. 47) contain the speeches of one character only with appropriate *cues*. A cue consists of the last few words of the previous speech (containing a stimulus word) which reminds the actor that the next speech

<pre>
             THE   PICK-POCKETS

                   MR. GREEN

                    ACT I

Take a seat, my dear fellows, and explain to me

exactly what your problem is.

                         ... would like a drink.

Oh! I'm sorry. Would you care for a sherry?

            (Nods from Bill, Mick and Tommy)

I'll just go and get some clean glasses.

                  (Exit left)

                         ... here he comes.

(Enter with four glasses. Begins to pour sherry)

Here we are chaps. Say when.

               (Hands them the drinks)

Now will you kindly state your business - I'm

a busy man, and Lady Cranbourne is expecting me

for lunch.

                         ... see her immediately.

I don't see how it can be arranged.
</pre>

Fig. 47.—*An actor's part*

or action is his. An actor's part is meant to be carried around in a pocket so that the actor may learn his words, and it must therefore be typed on a small piece of paper. When typing:

(a) Use A5-size paper and type on one side only, in double-line spacing (and double-line between speeches), with margins of ½in. at each side.

(b) The first page is headed with the name of the play, underneath which is centred the name of the character, in capitals. The Act number is also centred underneath, followed by the speeches of the character.

(c) The cues which separate the speeches begin at the middle of the page and are preceded by three or four dots.

(d) Only the stage directions applicable to the one character are included in the typing, and these are typed in single-line spacing.

(e) As with the complete play, all parts not actually spoken are typed in red, or underlined in red.

8. Programmes. Programmes can be typed on a sheet of A4-size paper, folded to make four pages. If it is for a play, the first three pages of the programme are typed as for the first three pages of the play proper (*see* **5** above), the last page may be left blank, or there may be the printer's name, or an acknowledgment. This can be centred horizontally and vertically, or it can be centred horizontally and placed near the bottom of the page.

Programmes for concerts (*see* Fig. 48) may also be typed on a folded sheet of paper, often with the contents typed across the total width of the two inside pages. Alternatively, the programme may be typed on a single sheet of paper. In either case, an ornamental border may be placed around the edge of the page, if desired.

When typing a concert programme there must be equal margins at the sides, and an equal space at the top and bottom of the page, and the following information should be clearly displayed:

(a) *Description of the item* (*e.g.* aria), typed in capitals.

(b) *Name of the item*, typed in lower case but enclosed by inverted commas.

(c) *Name of the artist*, typed in capitals.

(d) *Name of the composer*, typed in lower case and under-

BUSINESS TYPEWRITING

<u>THE JULIUS ORCHESTRAL SOCIETY</u>

<u>P R O G R A M M E</u>

OVERTURE	"The Silken Ladder"	<u>Rossini</u>
	THE ORCHESTRA	
ARIA	from "Madame Butterfly"	<u>Puccini</u>
	ELIZABETH LANGTON	
ARIA	from "The Marriage of Figaro"	<u>Mozart</u>
	GEORGE BULL	
DUET	from "The Magic Flute"	<u>Mozart</u>
	ELIZABETH LANGTON and GEORGE BULL	

I N T E R V A L

SYMPHONY	"The Eroica"	<u>Beethoven</u>

FIG. 48.—*A concert programme*

lined (indicating to the printer that it must be printed in italics). The last letter in the names of the composers should all finish at exactly the same point underneath each other, in order that the right-hand margin is perfectly straight. This will entail the use of the back-spacer when typing.

9. Poetry. Poetry is typed as follows:

(*a*) Use single-line spacing with equal margins at either side.

(*b*) Each line commences with a capital letter.

(*c*) If the poem or verse occurs in a general text (*e.g.* as a quotation in a literary report) it is centred over the line of writing, with two clear line-spaces separating it from the text. Quotation marks, if required, are placed at the beginning of the first verse and at the end of the last.

(*d*) If successive lines rhyme, or if there is no rhyme at all, each row commences at the margin.

EXAMPLE:
```
          Gone are those times of gentle leisure,
          When people drove abroad for pleasure.
          They're much too busy nowadays
          Courting death on motorways.
```

(*e*) If alternate lines rhyme, the second, fourth, etc., lines are indented two or three spaces.

EXAMPLE:
```
          I want to go home to Ireland,
            Where the lakes are fresh and free,
          Where the birds sing loud and clearly
            And the mountains reach the sea.
```

(*f*) If the rhyme follows no fixed pattern, the general rule is to indent any rhyming lines to the same point on the scale.

EXAMPLE:
```
          Water is a fickle creature
             Of changeable moods.
            In mountain tarns she darkly broods,
               Laughs aloud in hurrying streams,
          Then loses all control
             And screams
          And rages in the waterfall.
```

(*g*) The title is typed in capitals, centred over the line of writing, and separated from the verses by two or three clear line-spaces.

(h) The author's name is typed at the end of the poem and is preceded by a dash and one space. The name is underlined, and the last letter should be lined up with the last letter of the longest row in the poem.

(i) Leave two or three clear line-spaces between the verses.

(j) If a line of the verse is comparatively long, the last word or two may be placed above or below that line at the right-hand side. This is called a *hook-in*, and its use gives a more balanced effect to the overall appearance.

```
EXAMPLE:  There sits Mary, nose in book.
          While busy Marthas scrub and cook,
          Dust and polish, do the flowers,        / and hours,
          Mary sprawls in the big arm-chair for hours and hours
          Lost in a make-believe world of ivory towers.
```

(k) If a line is comparatively short, it may be commenced in the middle or a little before the middle of the row above.

```
EXAMPLE:  Her dress edged with a ruffle of foam,
          Silk-shot in the moon's gleams,
          Under the tranquil night sky
                    The sea dreams.
```

(l) The acute accent(')may be inserted on the syllable "ed" at the end of a verb (*i.e.* callèd) when this has to be pronounced in order to maintain the metre of the poem. The accent is normally written in by hand with pen and black ink (or ball-point pen) after the typing is completed. A complete poem is shown on p. 103.

VII. LITERARY WORK

<u>EXILE</u>

> I want to go home to Ireland,
>   Where the lakes run fresh and free,
> Where the birds sing loud and clearly,
>   And the mountains reach the sea.
>
> Where the farmer takes his cattle
>   Along the lanes to graze,
> In bright green fields Mc'Racken owns;
>   They've not been there for days.
>
> I had to leave my homeland
>   To seek for work elsewhere,
> So I went to another country,
>   Which, to me, seemed barren and bare.
>
> No more my native tongue to hear,
>   No more to hear the sound
> Of old Mc'Racken's cattle,
>   As homeward they are bound.
>
> Still I long to go home to Ireland,
>   Where the lakes run fresh and free,
> And my heart still yearns for the mountains
>   That reach down to the placid sea.
>
> — <u>K. Wasson</u>

PROGRESS TEST 7

1. Describe how:

    (*a*) a fair copy,

    (*b*) a draft copy,

is typed. (**1**)

2. How would you type the heading of a chapter? (**1**)

3. What do you understand by the following terms:

    (*a*) Short page.
    (*b*) Dropped heading.
    (*c*) Tail-piece.
    (*d*) Cue.
    (*e*) Hook-in. (**1, 7, 9**)

4. What are the positions of the quotation marks when quoting:

    (*a*) Prose.
    (*b*) Poetry? (**2**)

5. When several typists are typing a continuous document what points must be remembered? (**3**)

6. When correcting a printer's proof, what marks would be

inserted in the text and in the margin to indicate the following corrections:

    (*a*) Change to italic letters.
    (*b*) Straighten line.
    (*c*) Substitute good letter.
    (*d*) Put letter the right way up.
    (*e*) Change to roman type.
    (*f*) Equalise spacing between words. (**4**)

7. Give three different positions for the typing of the stage directions in a play. Explain when each position is used. (**5**)

8. Give general rules for the typing of an actor's part. (**7**).

9. When typing a concert programme, which items of information should be:

    (*a*) Underlined.
    (*b*) Typed in capitals? (**8**)

10. How should the following types of poem be typed:

    (*a*) With verses containing consecutive rhyming lines.
    (*b*) With verses containing alternate rhyming lines.
    (*c*) With verses containing no rhyming lines. (**9**)

The following programme will later be duplicated on A4 paper. One stencil will be used for the front and back covers and another for the inside sections. On two pieces of A4 paper inserted lengthwise in your machine, type a preparatory copy for the two stencils. (The A4 may, if necessary, be folded.)

Front Cover

CHILTONBURY SCHOOL ← Closed caps

THE ANNUAL CONCERT ← Spaced caps

1971

Thursday, Friday and Saturday
15th, 16th and 17th July

Programme 5p

Inside Left
(centre PROGRAMME over both inside pages in spaced caps.) (justified margin for names of composers)

CHOIR

The Jonah-Man Jazz .... Michael Hurd.
Denis Worth (saxophone/clarinet)
John Bray (trumpet)   George Cary (trombone)
Christopher Farmer (piano)
Peter Williams, Phillip May, John Griffiths
and Nigel Mee (drums)
Conductor: Stephen Bird

OBOE AND PIANO
Two Metamorphoses after Ovid .... Benjamin Britten
(i) Pan, who played upon the reed pipe which was Syrinx, his beloved.
(ii) Arethusa who, flying from the love of Alpheus the river god, was turned into a fountain.

Romance for Oboe and Piano Op. 94 ... Schumann
David Harvey (oboe) Tony Benson (piano)

INTERVAL

Inside Right

Music for Various Voices ← caps & centre

Lost is my quiet — — — — — — — — Purcell
Shepherd leave decoying — — — — — — "
  Colin Baker and David Griffin (trebles)
      Christopher Farmer (piano)
Feasting I watch — — — — — Edward Elgar
In the Mood — — — — — arr. John Walker
Sleepytime Bach — — — — arr. Bennett Williams
     Conductor: Stephen Bird

THE ORCHESTRA

Suite: "Le Roi s'amuse" — — — — — Léo Delibes,
                                   arr. A. W. Benoy
  Galliarde — Pavane — Scene du bouquet
  Lesquercarde — Passepied — Finale
Three pieces from "Swan Lake"   Tchaikovsky,
                                 arr. David Stone
  Scene — Dance of the Little Swans — Valse
     Conductor: Denis Worth

Back Cover

DATES TO NOTE

Sports Day   Tuesday 20th July
End of Summer Term   Friday 23rd   "
Autumn Term commences:
  Sixth form pupils Tuesday 7th Sept.
  New entrants   Wednesday, 8th "
  All the School   Thursday 9th "
Parent-Teacher Assn. Meeting — Wed. 29th "
Half Term Holiday   Mon. & Tues., 25th & 26th
                                    October.

VII. LITERARY WORK

School Play   Thurs. Fri. & Sat., 25th, 26th
Speech Day   Friday 27th November.
Carol Concert   Thurs. 16th December.
End of Autumn Term   Friday 17th Dec.
School Ski-ing Party departs Sunday 19th December
       "   "   returns Monday 27th Dec..

10.12.71

R.S.A.—ADVANCED 1971

CHAPTER VIII

LEGAL WORK

1. General rules. The typewriting of legal documents differs in several ways from general typewriting, and the following points should be carefully noted by the typist:

(*a*) Large-size paper of good quality is often used, and because of this it may be necessary to use a typewriter with a "brief"-size carriage—this is about 18in. long. A black record ribbon is also necessary, in order to eliminate possible smudges and fading.

(*b*) The first typing of a legal document is called the *draft copy*. It is typed as follows:

    (*i*) On A4 or foolscap paper.
    (*ii*) In treble-line spacing with wide margins. This is to allow for corrections to be made to the wording of the draft.
    (*iii*) On one side of the paper only.
    (*iv*) With abbreviations written in full, although dates, sums of money and other figures are left as figures (not spelt out as words).
    (*v*) With the word "draft" appearing before the title, at the beginning of the document.

(*c*) The second typing of the document is called the *fair copy* or *clean draft*. It is typed as follows:

    (*i*) On A4 or foolscap paper.
    (*ii*) In double-line spacing with wide margins.
    (*iii*) On one side of the paper only.
    (*iv*) With no abbreviations, and figures as in the draft copy.
    (*v*) With the words "fair copy" appearing at the beginning of the document.

(*d*) The final typing of the document, called the *engrossment*, is typed as follows (*see* Fig. 49):

    (*i*) Use A4-, A3-, draft- or brief-size paper, according to the type of document (*see* X, **10**).

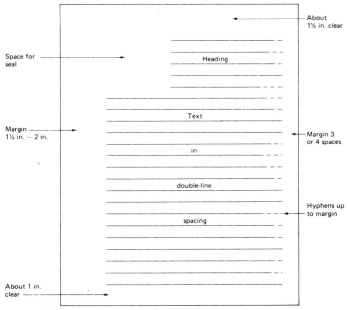

FIG. 49.—*Layout of the first page of a legal document*

(*ii*) Type in double-line spacing, with a wide margin at the left-hand side (twenty or twenty-four spaces), and a narrow margin at the right-hand side. This is to accommodate any ribbon or cord, or other method of fixing the sheets together.

(*iii*) The title of the document may be centred across the page, but sometimes it begins at the middle of the page (extending to the right-hand margin) in order to leave a blank space at the left-hand side for a seal, if necessary.

(*iv*) Type on both sides of the paper. When typing on the reverse side (*see* Fig. 50), it must be remembered that the right-hand margin should be as wide as the left-hand margin on the first page, in order to leave enough space for the ties; leave a narrower margin on the left-hand side.

(*v*) If the document is lengthy, two, three or more sheets of paper may be inserted inside each other (as for a book), and the typing carries on from one page to the next.

(vi) No abbreviations are allowed, and all names, dates, sums of money and figures (except house numbers) are typed in full (spelt out in words).

(vii) It is usual to omit punctuation marks, the sense of the document being maintained by the use of such phrases as "and whereas": punctuation marks, however carefully placed, might alter the meaning. Many of the words are typed in capitals, or spaced capitals, in order to make certain parts of the document stand out. Unspaced capitals are used at the beginning of clauses and for the names of the parties when first mentioned; spaced capitals are used for the name of the document and for the word "BETWEEN."

(viii) No erasures are allowed. If a correction were visible it could indicate that the document had been altered in some way. If an error occurs whilst typing the document, that page or pages must be retyped.

(ix) The typist may be required to fill up all blank spaces

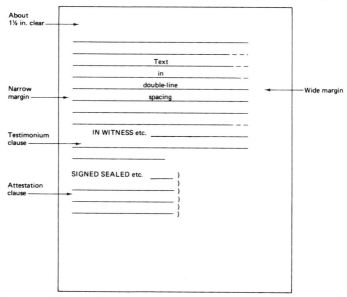

FIG. 50.—*Layout of a reverse page of a legal document, showing the position of the final clauses*

after the last word in a line, right up to the margin. This is to eliminate any possibility of words being added at a later date. The blanks can be filled in with dashes, or the underscore, or a neat line may be ruled in red after the typing is completed.
- (*x*) The pages are numbered at the bottom, in the centre, 1 in. being left clear below the figure.
- (*xi*) There must be no division of words at line-endings.
- (*xii*) The last page of the document is left blank for the typing of the endorsement (*see* **2**) after folding the document.
- (*xiii*) If a copy of a document is to be made, the word "copy" must be typed before the title, and the word "signed" placed in brackets before the typed name of the signatory.
- (*xiv*) If two engrossments are required for two different people (as opposed to one engrossment with a copy), one of the documents is called the *counterpart*.

2. Folding and endorsement. The engrossment is folded, and on the back page certain details are typed; this is the endorsement. The document can be folded in different ways according to the size of the paper and the number of pages.

(*a*) Foolscap and A4 paper may be folded vertically into two, or horizontally into four (*see* Fig. 51).
- (*i*) *To fold into two:* turn the left-hand edge to the right-hand edge and crease. The endorsement is now typed down the facing length.
- (*ii*) *To fold into four:* place the sheets face upwards; turn the bottom edges to meet the top, and crease; turn the folded edges to meet the top, and crease again; turn the document clockwise so that the lower folded edge is to the left; the endorsement is now typed down the facing length.

(*b*) Documents larger than foolscap size are generally folded into four, as explained above, but if they are very bulky only two folds may be possible.

The details of the endorsement should be typed down the length of the page, usually in the following order:
- (*i*) *The date.* Placed near the top, centred and sometimes underlined.
- (*ii*) *The names of the parties.* Placed at or near the middle of the page (lengthwise), centred, with each name on a separate line.
- (*iii*) *A brief description of the contents of the document.* Effectively displayed, perhaps using spaced capitals

it should be positioned about half-way between the names of the parties and the bottom of the sheet.

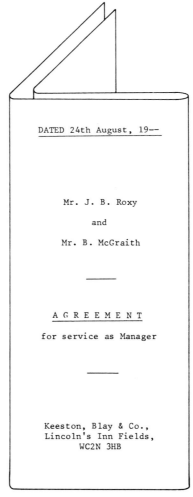

FIG. 51.—*An endorsement on a four-folded document*

VIII. LEGAL WORK 113

(iv) *The name and address of the solicitor.* Placed at the bottom, typed in either block or indented style.

If the document consists of only two pages (*i.e.* one sheet typed on the front and the reverse side), it is necessary to use a separate sheet of paper for the endorsement. If this is likely to arise, it is better to use a larger size of paper for the typing and fold it to make a four-page document.

When typing the endorsement on a four-folded document, it is best to open out the document for insertion into the machine and to type between the appropriate creases. Only the sheet to be typed on would be inserted.

3. Special clauses (*see* Fig. 50). The testimonium clause and the attestation clause, which are placed at the end of the document, are the clauses against which the interested parties and the witnesses sign their names.

The wording of these clauses may vary, but the testimonium clause usually begins "IN WITNESS whereof," and the attestation clause "SIGNED, SEALED AND DELIVERED." The clauses are generally typed at the left-hand side of the page, leaving at least half the page blank for the actual signatures; a brace can be typed at the right-hand side of the clauses.

4. Types of legal document.

(*a*) *An abstract of title* is a summary of the contents of various documents, and sets out evidence of ownership of real estate. Use brief-size paper.

(*b*) *An affidavit* is a written declaration given on oath before a magistrate or other person of authority. Use A4 or foolscap paper.

(*c*) *An assignment* is a document in which the transfer of any right or property is made. Use A3 or A4 paper.

(*d*) *A brief* is a document prepared by a solicitor for his client's defence counsel (in the law court) and contains a statement of the client's case. Use brief-size paper.

(*e*) *A deed or agreement* is a contract between two or more people. Choose your paper size according to the length of the document.

(*f*) *A disposition* is a document setting out the bestowal of property.

(*g*) *A lease* is a document dealing with the letting of

property or land. Choose your paper size according to the length of the document.

(*h*) *A statement of claim* is a document setting out the rights of a claimant. Choose your paper size according to the length of the document.

(*i*) *A statutory declaration* is a signed declaration. Use foolscap or A4 paper.

(*j*) *A will* is a document in which a person sets out the distribution and/or adminstration of his property, to take effect after his death. Choose your paper size according to the length of the document. A *holograph will* is a will written in a person's own handwriting.

5. Legal abbreviations. When typing a legal document from a manuscript copy there are likely to be many abbreviations. Some will be of general words, but others will be of less common words which neverthleess appear frequently in legal documents. Appendix I lists both general abbreviations and those likely to be found in a legal work.

PROGRESS TEST 8

1. Explain the following terms:

   (*a*) Draft copy.
   (*b*) Fair copy.
   (*c*) Engrossment.
   (*d*) Counterpart. (**1**)

2. Describe the method of typing an engrossment. (**1**)

3. Why are no erasures allowed in the final typing of a legal document? (**1**)

4. When typing a legal document, all blank spaces after the last word of a line must be filled in. Why is this? How should the blank spaces be filled? (**1**)

5. How are legal documents folded? (**2**)

6. What information is included when endorsing a legal document? (**2**)

7. Where and how should the testimonium and the attestation clauses be typed? (**3**)

8. Briefly describe the nature of the following legal documents:

   (*a*) Assignment.
   (*b*) Brief.
   (*c*) Affidavit.
   (*d*) Will. (**4**)

VIII. LEGAL WORK

Type one copy of the following on plain white paper. No ruling or underscoring required, other than that indicated.

VALUATION DATES

Valuation dates for the remainder of 1970 will be as follows:-

Valuation dates	Applications to contribute and notice of withdrawal to be received by	Securities offered to be notified by as contributions
17 June	10 June	3 June
22 July	15 July	8 July
19 August*	12 August	5 August
23 September	16 September	9 September
21 October	14 October	7 October
18 November	11 November	4 November
16 December	9 December	2 December

All correspondence and inquiries should be addressed to the Secretary of the Trust, from whom the necessary forms and further information may be obtained.

* Distribution Date

R.S.A.—ELEMENTARY 1971

CHAPTER IX

OTHER BUSINESS DOCUMENTS

1. General points about committee work. The copy typist, although not usually required to be present at a committee meeting, must be familiar with the layout of some of the documents connected with a meeting, especially notices, agendas and minutes. These are described in paragraphs **2, 3,** and **4** below.

2. Notices (*see* Fig. 52). The notice of a meeting must be sent to all committee members well before the actual date, and it must contain the following information, which should be effectively displayed on A4 or A5 paper:

(*a*) *The name of the company or body holding the meeting*, in block or spaced capitals, near the top of the page.

```
T H E    L O W T O W N    D O G - L O V E R S '    S O C I E T Y
```

                         A COMMITTEE MEETING

                            will be held at

                        THE CENTRAL HALL, LOWTOWN

                       on Saturday, 15th March, 19--

                             at 2.30 p.m.

                                                       J. Smith
             28th February, 19--   Secretary

FIG. 52.—*A notice for a meeting*

IX. OTHER BUSINESS DOCUMENTS 117

(b) *The kind of meeting*, typed in block capitals, and possibly underlined.

(c) *The place, date and time of the meeting*, typed in lower case and displayed on several lines.

(d) *The date the notice was sent out*, typed in the lower left-hand corner of the page, in lower case; the secretary's name and designation is typed on the right-hand side.

T H E   L O W T O W N   D O G - L O V E R S '   S O C I E T Y

COMMITTEE MEETING

to be held at the Central Hall, Lowtown,

on Saturday, 15th March, 19--, at 2.30 p.m.

A G E N D A

1. Minutes of the committee meeting held on
    Saturday, 3rd January, 19--.

2. Resignation of Mr. George Smithby.

3. Election of Treasurer.

4. The summer Dog Show.

5. Financial assistance for Mrs. G. B. Robertson,
    for the Paris Dog Show.

6. Date of next meeting.

7. Any other business.

FIG. 53.—*An agenda, with centred items*

T H E   L O W T O W N   D O G - L O V E R S '   S O C I E T Y

COMMITTEE MEETING

to be held at the Central Hall, Lowtown,

on Saturday, 15th March, 19--, at 2.30 p.m.

A G E N D A

1.	Minutes of the committee meeting held on Saturday, 3rd January, 19--.	))))
2.	Resignation of Mr. George Smithby.	))
3.	Election of Treasurer.	))
4.	The summer Dog Show.	))
5.	Financial assistance for Mrs. G. B. Robertson, for the Paris Dog Show.	))))
6.	Date of next meeting.	))
7.	Any other business.	)

FIG. 54.—*A Chairman's agenda*

3. Agendas (*see* Figs. 53 and 54). The agenda, which is a list of the items to be discussed at the meeting, is usually sent with the notice—this enables the members to think about the topics beforehand. It is typed on A4 paper in the following manner:

(*a*) The name of the company or body holding the meeting typed in capitals at the top of the page.

(*b*) The details of the meeting (the type of meeting, place, date, time, as they appeared in the notice) should be displayed on two or three lines, below the heading.

(*c*) The word "AGENDA" is then centred on the page, typed in spaced capitals.

(d) The topics for discussion are then listed down the page in the order in which they are to be discussed, and are typed as follows:
- (i) Double-line spacing between the items, but single-line spacing for individual items that occupy two or more rows.
- (ii) The list should be centred on the page.
- (iii) Alternatively, the list may be typed at the 1 in. left-hand margin, with each row finishing slightly to the right of the centre of the page. This leaves nearly half the page blank for the purpose of written notes taken during the course of the meeting. With this method a brace is typed down the whole length of the agenda, separating it from the blank portion (*see* X, **5** for the method of typing a brace). This style is used for the Chairman's agenda.

(e) Sometimes, especially if the agenda is rather short, the notice and agenda are combined to form one document. In this case, the name of the company, the type of meeting and the place, date and time are typed as displayed headings (as for the notice); and the agenda is typed below, in the manner described in (c) and (d) above.

4. Minutes (*see* Fig. 55). The minutes of a meeting are the official record of the proceedings, and are typed from shorthand or other notes taken during the actual meeting. A minute book is kept (often in the form of a loose-leaf binder), and each set of minutes is placed in this, after they have been approved by the members and signed by the Chairman.

The minutes are typed as described below:

(a) Use A4 paper, with a wide left-hand margin ($1\frac{1}{2}$ in.—2in.) and a normal right-hand margin (1in.).

(b) The heading, which consists of the same details as the heading of the agenda (*i.e.* name of company, type of meeting, place, etc.), is typed in one of two ways.
- (i) Displayed across the page as for the agenda (**3** (*a*) and (*b*)).
- (ii) In the form of a hanging paragraph (I, **14**), in single-line spacing, beginning about half-way across the page.

(c) A list of members present, beginning with the Chairman, is typed below the heading. This list is centred and typed in single-line spacing. If the list of members is very long (*e.g.* as would happen at an annual general meeting) it

M I N U T E S of the COMMITTEE MEETING

held at the Central Hall, Lowtown,

on Saturday, 15th March, 19--, at 2.30 p.m.

Present: Mr. J. Landy (Chairman)
          Mr. A. Green
          Mrs. B. Low
          Mrs. J. March
          Miss V. Orner
          Mr. J. Smith (Secretary)
          Mr. S. Williams
          Mr. G. Wood

Apologies: Miss S. Scott

MINUTES. The minutes of the committee meeting held on Saturday, 3rd January, 19--, were read by the Secretary, approved by all members and signed by the Chairman.

RESIGNATION. Deep regret was expressed by all members on hearing of the continued illness of Mr. George Smithby, necessitating his resignation from the post of Treasurer.

FIG. 55.—*Part of the first page of the minutes of a meeting*

IX. OTHER BUSINESS DOCUMENTS 121

is not necessary to type the name of every person present. The officers and committee members would be referred to by name, followed by the phrase "and . . . members"—the actual number being inserted where indicated.

(d) A list of apologies for absence is centred below the list of members present, typed in single-line spacing.

(e) The general text then begins, and the proceedings are typed in chronological order using single-line spacing (double between items).

Each description is preceded by a side-heading typed in capital letters. This heading may be a shoulder heading, *i.e.* the first three or four letters of the heading are typed in the margin. All shoulder headings should begin at the same point on the typewriter scale.

(f) If the minutes occupy more than one page, the second and following pages are numbered at the top of the sheet in the centre, the text continuing after two clear line-spaces.

5. Specifications (*see* Fig. 56). A specification is a statement of the work to be undertaken by a builder, an architect, an engineer or other similar type of person, and although companies may have individual preferences there are two styles of layout in general use. Both styles are divided into three parts: the heading, the side-headings and the body of the text. The only difference occurs in the way the heading is displayed. The important points to note when typing specifications are as follows:

(a) Use *A4 paper*, with a wide left-hand margin of twenty-five or thirty spaces, in order to accommodate the side-headings. A right-hand margin of ½in.—1in. is sufficient.

(b) The heading for a builder's or architect's specification is typed in *hanging paragraph form* (*see* I, **14**) and commences ½in.—1in. to the right of the left-hand margin, *i.e.* at about point 30–36 on the typewriter scale; second and subsequent lines are indented two or three spaces. The heading, which always begins with the word "SPECIFICATION" in spaced capitals, is typed in double-line spacing.

The heading for an engineer's specification is displayed across *the width of the page*, full use being made of capital letters and effective line-spacing.

(c) In a surveyor's or architect's specification, *the name and address* of the surveyor or architect is typed below the heading, separated from it by one clear line-space. It is typed in single-line spacing, in indented form (with each line indented five or six spaces), beginning at such a point that the last line of the address finishes at, or near, the right-hand margin.

(*d*) *The date is then typed at the left-hand margin*, one clear line-space separating it from the heading or, in the case of a surveyor's or architect's specification, from the name and address.

(*e*) The body of the specification, with the side-headings, is now typed. The body may be in *single or double-line spacing* (according to the length of the document) with indented or block paragraphs.

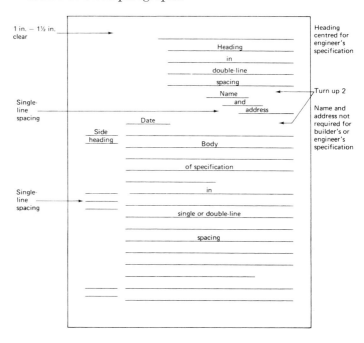

Fig. 56.—*Layout of an architect's or surveyor's specification*

IX. OTHER BUSINESS DOCUMENTS   123

The *side-headings are always typed in capitals, in single-line spacing*, and at about point 10 or 12 on the typewriter scale.

Any sub-headings which occur are centred over the line of writing, and are typed in spaced or block capitals, underlined if desired.

Specifications are often *endorsed* in the same way as legal documents (*see* VIII, **2**).

6. Bill of quantities (*see* Fig. 57). A bill of quantities is a summary of the work to be done by a builder; it gives full details and measurements, with a complete description of the building materials required. This document is necessary in order that the builder may make an accurate estimate of the price to be charged for any work he may undertake.

The bill is usually typed on ruled A4 or ruled foolscap paper but the typist may have to type on plain paper and insert the ruled lines in pen and ink after the typing is completed.

The first sheet should bear the name and address of the builder, and underneath this is typed the heading. This is typed in double-line spacing, in hanging paragraph form, and is centred over the whole page. The heading commences with the words "BILL OF QUANTITIES" which is typed in spaced capitals and underlined; the rest of the heading, which may be several lines in length, is typed in lower case. Second and subsequent sheets are plain (except for the ruling), and are numbered in the centre at the top.

The columns are as follows:

(*a*) *The first three columns*, which are narrow, are for measurement figures. Headings are not necessary, as the type of measurement may vary from one item to the next, *e.g.* one item may be measured in yards, feet and inches, and the next item may be in rods, feet and inches, or different metric units may be used. The abbreviations for "yards," etc., are typed immediately above the figure to which they refer, and no other heading would be inserted until a change occurs in that particular column.

(*b*) *The fourth column* (also narrow) is used for describing the nature of the measurements, *e.g.* superficial (typed as "sup"), cubic (typed as "cube").

(*c*) *The fifth column* is the descriptive column and should be made as wide as possible. Each item is described in turn

BILL OF QUANTITIES of WORK to be performed in the erection of a dwelling house to be known as 49 Grove Avenue, Compton Town, GL6 10D

EXCAVATOR AND BRICKLAYER

	Feet				£	p.
Yds 90	2	–	sup.	Remove top soil and place at side of site		
40	–	–	cube	Excavate trenches and fill with concrete (as described)		
Rods 32	98	–	sup.	Reduced brickwork in cement mortar		

FIG. 57.—*Part of the first page of a bill of quantities*

BALANCE SHEET

as at 31st December, 19—

Liabilities	£	Assets	£
Capital subscribed and paid up	500,000	Cash in hand and at bank	750,000
Reserve fund	275,000	Money at call	200,000
Current and deposit accounts	3,375,500	Investments	1,754,280
Profit and loss account	112,600	Loans and advances	1,433,820
		Premises	125,000
	£4,263,100		£4,263,100

FIG. 58.—*A simple balance sheet*

RECEIPTS AND PAYMENTS

FOR YEAR ENDED 31st DECEMBER, 19--

Receipts				Payments		
	£	£			£	£
Balance in hand and at bank		75.00		Stationery	10.05	
				Printing	22.35	
Subscriptions	324.00			Postage	49.05	81.45
Donations	25.50					
Coffee evenings	22.45	371.95		Advertising		15.00
Interest deposit account		5.00		Rent	150.00	
				Rates	45.00	195.00
Profit from jumble sale		41.25				
				Cleaner's wages		52.00
				Sundry expenses		12.50
				Balance		137.25
		£493.20				£493.20

Fig. 59.—*A balance sheet with four money columns*

and is typed in single-line spacing in indented, block or hanging paragraph form. One clear line-space separates each item, and leader dots may be inserted if the last line of a description is short.

(d) *The sixth column* is the "rate" column, *i.e.* showing the rate at which the item is priced.

(e) *The last two columns* are the money columns, for the insertion of the price of each item. The columns are totalled at the foot of each page and the balance brought forward to the next page; a final total is entered at the end of the document.

When the typist is required to hand-rule the paper, the positions for the ruled lines must be calculated as for any tabular statement (*see* V).

If the bill of quantities is for a large project, each trade would have a separate sheet, *e.g.* one sheet for the bricklayer, one for the plumber, etc., and the final sheet would summarise the whole, with a grand total made up of all the individual totals. This sheet would then be headed "SUMMARY," and the individual sheets would be headed with the name of each trade.

If the bill of quantities is for a small project, all the trades would be listed in one document, the names of the trades appearing as sub-headings centred over the descriptive column.

7. Balance sheets (*see* Fig. 58). The sizes of a balance sheet can vary a great deal, and therefore it may be typed on any size of paper from A4 to brief-size. Two sheets of A4 or foolscap paper may be joined together, after typing the two sides of the balance sheet separately, if a typewriter with a brief-size carriage is not available.

The simplest form of balance sheet consists of four columns —a descriptive column and a money column on each side of the sheet (the left-hand one is the debit side and the right-hand one is the credit side). A ruled line may be inserted down the centre of the page after the typing is completed. The positions for the commencement of typing of the various columns are calculated as for any tabular statement (*see* V).

The sides of the sheet are typed alternately until one side is completed except for the total, then the other is continued until the end; both totals are then typed at the same level.

More complicated balance sheets (*see* Fig. 59) may have four or more money columns (two or more each side), in addition to the descriptive columns. When this arises, the amounts entered in the first money column are added together at various points and their totals entered in the second money column. The typist shows this by underlining the figures in the first money column (at the point where they are added together), turning up the paper half a line-space, and then entering the total in the second money column.

When it is necessary to type the two sides of the balance sheet on separate sheets of paper, great care must be taken to make sure that the heading is arranged centrally across both sheets, and meets in the middle at exactly the same point. The two final totals must also be typed at exactly the same level, so it is advisable first to type the side which contains the most items, and then mark the position of the final total on the other sheet with a light pencil mark. The two sheets are joined together by an adhesive strip on the back after typing.

PROGRESS TEST 9

1. What information is necessary on a notice of a meeting? (**2**)
2. Describe the layout required for a Chairman's agenda. (**3**)
3. What are the minutes of a meeting? How should they be typed? (**4**)
4. List the parts of a specification. (**5**)
5. Describe the method of typing the heading for:

    (*a*) A builder's or architect's specification.

    (*b*) An engineer's specification. (**5**)
6. Draw a rough diagram showing a typical layout of a specification, including side-headings and sub-headings. (**5**)
7. What information is given in a bill of quantities? Why is this document necessary? (**6**)
8. How many columns of typing are required on a bill of quantities? What details are inserted in each column? (**6**)
9. What sizes of paper might you use when typing balance sheets? (**7**)
10. Describe briefly the method of layout of a balance sheet containing two or more money columns on each side of the paper, when no brief-size typewriter is available. (**7**)

On plain paper, type the following advance notice of a meeting. The typing is to fit on to a postcard 6" x 3½" and you should indicate this size by appropriate marking around your typing.

BRITISH SOCIETY OF CRAFTSMEN

NOTICE

A General Meeting will be held at THE DRILL HALL, COLWYN BAY, NORTH WALES, on Saturday, 18th July, 1970 at 10.30 a.m., and it is hoped you will be able to attend. The Agenda & other papers will be sent to you in the course of a few days time.

Secretary.

On a separate piece of paper, but occupying the same amount of indicated space (6" x 3½"—representing the reverse side of the card) type the address given below. Once again, the size of the card should be indicated.

Major Raymond Billinghurst,
16 Castle Hill Avenue,
St. Leonards-on-Sea,
Sussex.

Type one copy of the following Agenda.

BRITISH SOCIETY OF CRAFTSMEN

AGENDA - Sp.caps.

for the General Meeting to be held at

THE DRILL HALL, COLWYN BAY, NORTH WALES,

on Saturday, 18th July, 1970, at 10.30 a.m.

u.c. 1. Minutes of last general meeting.

2. Balance Sheet for 1969.

3. Alterations to Rules + Standing Orders:

    (b) Rule VII (paragraph 4)

        That the 1st line + the 1st 2 words in the second line be deleted, + the following inserted:-

        The ordinary member of each Branch Committee shall be nominated + elected at an Annual Branch Meeting.

    (a) Rule VII (para. 2)

l.c.   That Rule VII in so far as it concerns the Constitution of the Administrative Council be amended to read:-

l.c.   1. COUNCIL - The general Management of the affairs of the Society shall be vested in the Council which shall consist of 10 full members to be elected at the A.G.M. A fee of one guinea shall be paid to ea. member for ea. attendance. *(Annual General Meeting)*

4. Any other business.

5. Date of next meeting.

R.S.A.—INTERMEDIATE 1970

Type one copy of the following letter on headed paper, inserting today's date. One carbon copy is required on the yellow paper provided.

Dear Miss Freeman,

As promised, I send you the verses you wanted. They are:-

A SONG TO THE GARDENERS

We have many songs about the gardens,
   Of the roses and the trees,
Of dewy dawns and sunny lawns
   And scents in the evening breeze;
Birds are heard in the gardens
   'Mid a thousand blossoms bright.
But do we forget the work and sweat
   That bring such great delight?

Let us sing on about the gardens
   And extol them more and more,
For their loveliness, we do confess,
   Is here for us to adore.
But just once in a while, friends,
   As we honour these fair lands,
It is good again to sing refrain
   To the gardeners' brains and hands.

I thoroughly enjoyed the dinner on Saturday evening — the food was delicious + it was delightful meeting so many old friends again.

With best wishes,

Miss Josephine Freeman,
62 Elphinstone Road,
Yarmouth, I.O.W.

CHAPTER X

MISCELLANEOUS TYPEWRITING PROCEDURES

1. Division of words at line-endings. Division of words at the end of a line is sometimes necessary so that the right-hand margin is kept as even as possible. Divisions should not be too frequent, however, as this can be distracting for the reader. The typist should follow these general rules when dividing words:

(*a*) You should divide:
  (*i*) According to the pronunciation of the word, with the hyphen between two syllables, *e.g.* tor-toise.
  (*ii*) After a prefix or before a suffix, *e.g.* con-cept, enjoy-ment.
  (*iii*) At the normal hyphen in compound words, *e.g* co-opt.
  (*iv*) Between consonants which are doubled, *e.g.* let-ter.
  (*v*) So that the second part of the word begins with a consonant, if possible.
  (*vi*) Before "-ing," unless the previous letter is doubled, *e.g.* find-ing, *but* get-ting.
  (*vii*) After the first of three consonants occurring in the middle of a word, *e.g.* chil-dren.

(*b*) You should not divide:
  (*i*) Words of one syllable and their plurals (even though the plurals may consist of more than one syllable, *e.g.* house, houses).
  (*ii*) Proper names, groups of figures or sums of money.
  (*iii*) The last word in a paragraph, or the last word on a page.
  (*iv*) On more than two consecutive lines.
  (*v*) So that only two letters are carried over to the second line—the hyphen on the first line takes up one space, which could be occupied by one of the two letters carried over, and one letter more will not make a great deal of difference to the margin.
  (*vi*) Abbreviations or contractions.

2. Spacing after punctuation. There are several acceptable methods of spacing after punctuation marks, and whichever method you choose you must keep to it strictly—there must be no inconsistency whatever in a piece of work. The number of spaces allowed in the various methods are shown below:

In method:	1	2	3	4
Spaces left after:				
Comma	1	1	1	1
Semi-colon	1	2	2	1
Colon	1	2	2	2
Full stop	2	3	2	2

3. Time, money and quantities. The way these are typed may differ, according to whether the figures are in a column, or within the general text. When typing columns of figures, full use should be made of the tabulator stop.

(a) *Time.* Here are some examples of the various methods of expressing time:

(i) 0900 hours.
(ii) 9 a.m.
(iii) nine o'clock.

When typing times as in (i), it is essential that the first 0 is inserted for times before 1000 hours; after 1259 hours, the time is 1300 hours, etc.

When times are typed in a column, the style of (i) or (ii) may be used, but care must be taken to see that units are under units, tens under tens, etc. One space is left after the figure, and no space between a. and m.

EXAMPLE: 4 a.m.
10 a.m.
 6 p.m.
11 p.m.

(b) *Money.* Within a general text, money is usually expressed in figures, *e.g.* £16.50; but some documents (for example, legal documents, cheques) require the amounts to be written in words and figures.

If the £ sign is used, it is not necessary to insert "p" for the pence. Small amounts of money may be typed either as £0.45, or as 45p. If the amount is a whole number of pounds, it may be simply typed as £10, rather that £10.00.

When typing a column of money, the £ sign is inserted as a heading, and only the figures appear below it, with units under units, tens under tens, etc. If the column is totalled:

- (*i*) Underscore the last set of figures (without turning up).
- (*ii*) Turn up two single-line spaces, and then type the total with the £ sign to the left of the amount (outside the column).
- (*iii*) Turn up one single-line space and underscore again; one clear line-space is now left above and below the total.
- (*iv*) Using the variable line-spacer turn up the platen slightly and underscore again—this double line is normally used for a final total.

    The underscoring must not project beyond the furthermost figures to the left and right of the column. The £ sign at the left is not underscored.

EXAMPLE: £
            10·40
             2·90
           162·05
             0·95
           ───────
         £176·30
         ═══════

(*c*) *Quantities.* Quantities are often expressed in figures with the units of measurement in abbreviated form. The abbreviations, in., cwt, lb, oz, ft, m, mm, cm, km, kg, g, do not have an "s" added for plurals. In a general text, one space is left between the last figure and the word or abbreviation, *e.g.* 6 lb 4 oz.

When typed in columns, the unit of measurement is typed as the heading (in abbreviated form) and only the figures appear below it, again with tens under tens, etc.

EXAMPLE: ft. in.
             6   2
            10   10

4. Hyphen and dash. Misuse of the hyphen key is a common typwriting error.

(*a*) When the key is used to type a hyphen (*i.e.* to join compound words), no space is left on either side, except of

X. MISCELLANEOUS TYPEWRITING PROCEDURES 135

course, when the hyphen is written at the right-hand margin to divide a word when the margin space will be to the right of the hyphen.

(b) When the key is used to type a dash, indicating a pause, one space should be left on either side of the hyphen.

(c) When the key is used to indicate "to", as in 1964–65, there should be no space left on either side of the hyphen.

5. Combination signs. Combination signs are formed by the use of two or more typewriting characters. The characters may be superimposed (using the back-spacer) or, in some cases, the variable line-spacer is used.

The table on pp. 136–137 shows common combination signs and other special characters, and the way to form them.

6. Extra characters. The extra characters on the keyboard are used as follows:

(a) *Quotation mark* (").

    (*i*) Direct quotation.
    (*ii*) Names of books, plays, ships, etc.
    (*iii*) Inches and seconds.
    (*iv*) Ditto sign.
    (*v*) Umlaut and diaeresis.

(b) *Oblique* (/).

    (*i*) Combination signs.
    (*ii*) Abbreviation for "the."
    (*iii*) Sloping fractions.
    (*iv*) Separating two words, *e.g.* and/or.

(c) *"At" sign* (@).

Used only in the typing of invoices, and other commercial documents, to represent the word "at," meaning "at the rate of." No full stop is required after the sign.

(d) *£ sign* (**£**).

Used only to denote pounds (money), it is not followed by a full stop.

(e) *Ampersand* (**&**).

An abbreviation meaning "and," which is not followed by a full stop, and is used in:

    (*i*) Names of firms or businesses.
    (*ii*) An address involving two numbers, *e.g.* Nos. 6 & 8.

Combination Signs

Asterisk	✱	Use small x and hyphen.
Brace	( ) or)) ( )	Type one bracket, turn up one line-space. Back-space once, then type the next bracket.
Caret	∠	Type the oblique, back-space once, type the underscore.
Cedilla	ς	Type a small c, back-space once, type a comma.
Cent	ȼ	Type a small or capital C, back-space once, type an oblique.
Dagger	╪	Type a capital I, back-space once, type the hyphen.
Double dagger	╪╪	Type a capital I. Using the variable line-spacer slightly raise the line of typing, back-space once, type another capital I.
Degrees	o	Type a small o slightly raised above the line of typing.
Diaeresis and Umlaut	¨	Use quotation marks, raised above the line of typing. Back-spacing is necessary to position them above the correct letter.
Division	÷	Type a hyphen, back-space once, type a colon.
Dollar	$	Type a capital S, back-space once, type the oblique.
Equals	=	Type a hyphen. Using the variable line-spacer slightly raise the line of typing, back-space once and type the second hyphen.

X. MISCELLANEOUS TYPEWRITING PROCEDURES

Exclamation	!.	Type an apostrophe, back-space once, type a full stop.
Feet and Minutes	'	Use the apostrophe.
Inches and seconds	"	Use the quotation mark.
Per cent	°/o	Using the variable line-spacer slightly raise the line of typing, type a small o. Return to normal line of typing and type the oblique and the second o.
Section mark	§	Type a capital or small S. Using the variable line-spacer slightly raise the line of typing, back-space once, type the second S.
Square brackets	[ ]	For the left-hand bracket type the oblique, back-space once, type the lower underscore. Turn back the platen one line-space, type the upper underscore.
		For the right-hand bracket type the oblique, back-space twice, type the lower underscore. Turn back the platen one line-space, type the upper underscore.

(*iii*) Some abbreviations; *see* list in Appendix I.

(*f*) *Apostrophe* (').

(*i*) Omission of a letter in a word: don't.
(*ii*) Possessive case: Joan's book.
(*iii*) Indirect quotation.
(*iv*) Feet and minutes.
(*v*) Plurals of letters and figures, *e.g.* two b's.
(*vi*) Combination signs.

7. Roman numerals.

(*a*) The Roman numerals are as follows:

$$\begin{array}{ll} I = 1 & L = 50 \\ V = 5 & C = 100 \\ X = 10 & D = 500 \\ & M = 1000 \end{array}$$

A stroke written above a numeral multiplies that numeral by 1000, *e.g.* $\bar{D} = 500,000$.

(*b*) All other numbers are formed by dividing up the number you require into groups containing a combination of the numbers 1, 5, etc. listed above.

EXAMPLES:
$$\begin{aligned} 2 &= 1 + 1 \\ 3 &= 1 + 1 + 1 \\ 4 &= 5 - 1 \\ 9 &= 10 - 1 \\ 40 &= 50 - 10 \\ 68 &= 50 + 10 + 5 + 1 + 1 + 1 \\ 236 &= 100 + 100 + 10 + 10 + 10 + 5 + 1 \\ 949 &= (1000 - 100) + (50 - 10) + (10 - 1) \end{aligned}$$

It will be seen from these examples that 4 is always treated as (5–1), 9 as (10–1). This rule applies for any number containing 4 or 9, so $24 = (25-1)$, $29 = (30-1)$.

(*c*) When the number has been split up, each part is converted into roman numerals. The numerals are then written or typed side by side, with the highest number placed first, except in the case of the numbers containing 4 or 9, when the part to be subtracted is written first.

EXAMPLES:
$$\begin{aligned} 2 &= 1 + 1 = I + I = II \\ 3 &= 1 + 1 + 1 = I + I + I = III \\ 4 &= 5 - 1 = V - I = IV \\ 9 &= 10 - 1 = X - I = IX \end{aligned}$$

$$40 = 50 - 10 = L - X = XL$$
$$68 = 50 + 10 + 5 + 1 + 1 + 1 = L + X$$
$$+ V + I + I + I = LXVIII$$
$$236 = 100 + 100 + 10 + 10 + 10 + 5 + 1$$
$$= C + C + X + X + X + V + I$$
$$= CCXXXVI$$
$$949 = (1000 - 100) + (50 - 10) + (10 - 1)$$
$$= (M - C) + (L - X) + (X - I)$$
$$= CMXLIX$$

(*d*) Capital roman numerals are used in the following cases:

- (*i*) Numbering chapters, and acts of plays.
- (*ii*) Monarchs, *e.g.* Henry VIII.
- (*iii*) The year (usually only found in inscriptions).
- (*iv*) Occasionally for numbering paragraphs.
- (*v*) Class and form numbers.
- (*vi*) Books of the Bible.

(*e*) Small roman numerals are used in the following cases:

- (*i*) Numbering pages of a preface or introduction of a book.
- (*ii*) Numbering sub-paragraphs or sub-sections.

8. Ornamentation. Ornamental borders and corner pieces may be used for programmes or menus, and occasionally around notices. Some simple examples are shown below.

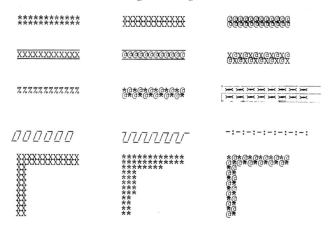

9. Types of paper. There are several types and sizes of paper available for office use, but those most often used are as follows:

(a) *Bond:* a good quality paper used for top copies. The sheets often have a watermark; this can be seen by holding the paper up to the light. The motif is seen the correct way round when looking at the top surface of the paper; if the motif is "mirrorwise" the wrong side of the paper is being looked at. The correct side, which is smoother than the reverse, can be ascertained from the watermark.

(b) *Bank:* a cheaper, much thinner paper, used for carbon copies. This paper is sometimes called "flimsy."

(c) *Duplicating:* absorbent paper used for the ink duplicating process.

10. Stationery sizes and uses.

Name	Size	Uses
A3	420 mm $\times$ 297 mm ($16\frac{1}{2}$ in. $\times$ $11\frac{3}{4}$ in.)	Balance sheets, legal documents.
A4	297 mm $\times$ 210 mm ($11\frac{3}{4}$ in. $\times$ $8\frac{1}{4}$ in.)	Correspondence, literary work, agendas, minutes, reports, menus, specifications, tabular work, commercial documents, bills of quantities.
A5	210 mm $\times$ 148 mm ($8\frac{1}{4}$ in. $\times$ $5\frac{7}{8}$ in.)	Memos, correspondence, actors' parts, short commercial documents (*e.g.* credit notes), notices, menus.
A6	148 mm $\times$ 105 mm ($5\frac{7}{8}$ in. $\times$ $4\frac{1}{8}$ in.)	Postcards, receipts, itineraries, advertisements, acknowledgment notes.
A7	105 mm $\times$ 74 mm ($4\frac{1}{8}$ in. $\times$ $2\frac{7}{8}$ in.)	Business cards, labels.
Brief	406 mm $\times$ 330 mm (16 in. $\times$ 13 in.)	Balance sheets, legal documents.
Draft	406 mm $\times$ 254 mm (16 in. $\times$ 10 in.)	Legal documents.
Foolscap (Fcp.)	330 mm $\times$ 203 mm (13 in. $\times$ 8 in.)	Reports, specifications, bills of quantities, some tabular work.
Quarto (4to. or Qto.)	254 mm $\times$ 203 mm (10 in. $\times$ 8 in.)	Correspondence, literary work, agendas, minutes, tabular work, commercial documents, menus.
Sixmo (6mo.)	203 mm $\times$ 164 mm (8 in. $\times$ $6\frac{1}{2}$ in.)	Correspondence.
Octavo (8mo.)	203 mm $\times$ 127 mm (8 in. $\times$ 5 in.)	Memos, correspondence, actors' parts, short commercial documents, menus, notices.

Name	Size	Uses
Postcard	139 mm × 88 mm (5½ in. × 3½ in.)	Advertisements, acknowledgment notes, itineraries.
Post Office Preferred Envelopes (P.O.P.)	Maximum: 235 mm × 121 mm (9¼ in. × 4¾ in.) Minimum. 140 mm × 89 mm (5½ in. × 3½ in.)	Envelopes outside these limits are liable to incur additional postal charges.

PROGRESS TEST 10

1. Give the rules for the division of words at line-endings. (**1**)
2. State three different ways of expressing the same time of day. (**3**)
3. When might it be necessary to type sums of money in words? (**3**)
4. Describe how you would type a column of money which includes a ruled total. (**3**)
5. Misuse of the hyphen and the dash is a common typewriting error. How should these be typed? (**4**)
6. What is a combination sign? List as many of these as you can and describe how they are typed. (**5**)
7. What are the uses of the following extra characters:
   (*a*) Quotation marks.
   (*b*) Oblique.
   (*c*) Ampersand.
   (*d*) Apostrophe. (**6**)
8. Write the following numbers in Roman numerals: 10, 40, 100, 162, 945, 1001, 1972. (**7**)
9. When would you use:
   (*a*) Capital roman numerals.
   (*b*) Small roman numerals? (**7**)
10. What sizes of paper are used for the following documents?
   (*a*) Literary work.
   (*b*) Credit notes.
   (*c*) Small balance sheets.
   (*d*) Tabular work.
   (*e*) Itineraries.
   (*f*) General correspondence.
   (*g*) Menus.
   (*h*) Actors' parts. (**10**)

Type this letter on headed paper for despatch today. Use A4 headed and take a carbon copy on the yellow paper supplied.

Mr. C. J. Price,
91b West Common Road,
HASTINGS,
Sussex.

Dear Colin,

Many thanks for yr. recent letter. We do still hold quite large stocks of octavo, quarto & foolscap paper & the prices of these remain unchanged for the time being. I sent you the price list a few months ago — if you need any of these sizes I suggest that you let us have the order fairly soon — I

N.P. have no doubt that the cost will go up in about a month's time. I am glad to hear that you are thinking of switching to the new sizes of paper. The International Organisation for Standardisation (ISO) aims to standardise the sizes of paper used for typing or printing throughout the world. These ISO sizes are based on the principle that any sheet cut or folded in half provides the next size down the series, eg, a sheet of A4 cut in half gives 2 sheets of A5.

The sizes you are most likely to need in your own office are:-

	mm	Uses
A4	210 x 297	headed notepaper, reports
A5	148 x 210	headed notepaper, memoranda
A6	105 x 148	postcards
A7	74 x 105	compliments slips, business cards

I suggest that you order a stock of A4 which you can then guillotine to A5 etc. (Prices vary between 43½p and 53p per ream). Ink duplicating paper is a little dearer (from 63p per ream) and we can supply white, blue, pink, buff, mauve, gold, green, & yellow.

Next time you are in London, please give me a ring & we can arrange to lunch together.

With best wishes,
Yours sincerely,

R.S.A.—ELEMENTARY 1971

CHAPTER XI

COPYING AND DUPLICATING

1. Methods of copying. Most work undertaken by a typist in a business or firm needs to be recorded in some way and a large number of copies are often required for circulation. A common method of producing copies of general work is to make *carbon copies* using carbon paper. Copies of circulars, handbills, notices, etc., of which large quantities may be required, can be reproduced on a *duplicator*, which may be a rotary or ink duplicator, a spirit duplicator, or an offset lithograph duplicator. All these machines require a "master," and the typist must know how to prepare the master and how to produce the copies. If only a few copies are required, a photographic copying machine may be used.

Some of the most common methods of copying and duplicating are described in **2** to **6** below.

2. Carbon copying. Up to six carbon copies can be produced on a manual typewriter with a medium-hard platen, and up to twenty copies on an electric typewriter. There are several grades of carbon paper (according to thickness and quality) and to produce good carbon copies a good grade of carbon paper must be used. When making the choice of the type of carbon paper, the points to be borne in mind are the number of copies required; the kind of typewriter being used (*e.g.* small portable, standard, manual, electric); the quality required of the copies; the thickness of the copy-paper.

Double-coated carbon paper is also available, with both sides of the sheet carbon-coated; this can be used when a large number of copies (up to thirty) are needed. The typist inserts two sheets of very thin (almost transparent) plain paper for each sheet of double-sided carbon paper and types in the normal manner. When the papers are removed each sheet will have a copy on it, but one sheet of each pair will have a negative impression. Because the paper is so thin, the words on this sheet can be read (the correct way round) simply by turning the paper over.

Carbon paper can be obtained in several sizes and colours, although black is the most commonly used. It can also be obtained in a roll instead of in separate sheets, and this is used in a continuous-stationery machine for multiple production of invoices, etc. When used for this purpose, it is very thinly coated with carbon and is normally used only once—hence the name "one-time carbon."

(a) *Handling and storage.* The handling and storage of carbon paper is very important, and the following points should be noted:

(i) Handle the carbon paper as little as possible, in order to avoid rubbing off the carbon. When it is necessary to handle it, hold it lightly by the edges.

(ii) Do not let eraser dust adhere to the carbon—after rubbing out, make sure all dust is blown away.

(iii) Store the carbon papers in a flat box, away from heat or sun. Never fold the carbon paper, as this causes "treeing," (creasing) which makes marks on any future copies.

(iv) Take care when feeding the carbon paper into the typewriter to avoid creasing it.

(v) Carbon paper can be used several times (except one-time carbons), and when using the same sheet a second time it should be turned upside-down or moved slightly to the right or left, to ensure that all the available carbon coating is being used; the sheet will then last longer than if the same portion of carbon coating is continually being worn off.

(b) *Making good carbon copies.* To produce really good carbon copies, the actual typing is as important as the carbon paper. The typewriter must also be of a suitable size to take the required number of copies, with clean type which is in good condition. A fairly hard platen which is free of ridges should also be used for a large number of copies, as this will provide a firm base on to which the typebars can strike. When only one copy is being taken, the use of a backing sheet will give a better copy, and this will also prolong the life of the typewriter ribbon, especially if the typewriter has a hard platen.

Having chosen the grade of carbon paper, and having collected together the top sheet (good quality typewriting paper), the required number of "flimsies" (sheets of thinner

XI. COPYING AND DUPLICATING 145

copying paper often of different colours for different departments), and the carbons, the procedure is as follows:

(*i*) Lay the top sheet face downwards on the table; place one sheet of carbon paper, with carbon coating upwards, on the top sheet; place one flimsy on top of the carbon paper. Place another carbon sheet (carbon coating upwards) and another flimsy on top of this. Repeat for the required number of copies, finishing with a flimsy.

(*ii*) Collect the sheets together and gently "knock" them into position, taking care not to rub the sheets together and handling them by the edges only.

(*iii*) Insert all the sheets into the machine, making sure that, when they are first placed at the back of the platen, the carbon surfaces are facing the typist. When the sheets are rolled around to the typing position, the carbon surfaces will be facing away from the typist.

(*iv*) It may prove difficult to insert a very large number of sheets together, and in this case, the best plan is to insert the top sheet with all the flimsies, and roll on the platen very slightly so that the sheets are just gripped. Then separate the sheets one by one and insert one sheet of carbon paper (carbon surface towards the typist) between each sheet of typewriting paper. Roll the platen on till the typing position is reached, and it will be seen that the tops of the copies do not have carbon paper underneath them —this is unimportant, as the very top of the paper is seldom typed on.

(*v*) Continue typing in the normal way, striking the keys smoothly and evenly, as any unevenness is more obvious on the carbon copy than on the top sheet. Punctuation marks should be struck rather more lightly than usual.

(*c*) *The correction of errors.* This can be a lengthy task, especially if a large number of copies is being made. To correct an error:

(*i*) Roll the platen forward about 1 in. from the error.

(*ii*) Insert a small piece of paper between each carbon and its copy, at the position of the error.

(*iii*) Move the carriage to the left or right.

(*iv*) Erase the top copy, then erase each carbon copy in turn. It may be easier to erase the carbons with a soft rubber instead of the normal typewriting rubber.

(*v*) When correcting the carbon copies, care must be taken not to smudge the print.

(vi) Remove all the small pieces of paper, return the carriage and roll the platen to the typing position. Type the correction, and proceed with the typewriting.

If an error is noticed after the papers have been removed from the machine, erase the error on each sheet of paper and then insert one sheet at a time into the machine, in order to type the correction. The alignment scale and variable line-spacer will probably have to be used to line up the typewriting exactly. The top copy will be typed in the normal way, but the carbon copies must have a slip of carbon paper inserted between the paper and the ribbon when typing the correction—this will ensure that the correction has the same appearance as the rest of the typing.

(d) *Other points to note*
- (i) If a note is to appear on the top copy and not on the carbon copies, insert small pieces of paper between each carbon and its copy at the correct position, and then type the note. The note will not then appear on the carbon copies.
- (ii) If a note is to appear on the carbon copy only (*i.e.* not on the top copy), insert it, using the following method, after all the sheets have been removed. Make a pencil mark on a plain, spare piece of paper at the correct position for the typing of the note. Place this, with a sheet of carbon paper, on the carbon copy on which the note has to be written. Insert all sheets in the typewriter and type the note at the position marked. The note on the carbon copy will then be typed in the same media as the rest of the copy, and this will improve the appearance. The plain, spare, piece of paper is then discarded.
- (iii) Carbon paper is often supplied with two corners snipped off, and this facilitates the separation of the carbon paper from the copies after completion of the typing. Hold the top sheet and copies by the corners, shake them and the carbon sheets will fall out.
- (iv) If there are any smudges on the carbon copies, they may be erased using a soft rubber. This is best done after the sheets are removed from the machine.
- (v) After completion of all the work requiring carbon copies, replace the carbon sheets carefully in their box—never leave them lying around on the desk.

3. Ink duplicating. Up to 5000 good copies may be produced on a rotary ink duplicator, using a special wax stencil as a master. The copies, which may be multi-coloured, are printed on absorbent duplicating paper which can be obtained in several sizes.

The principle of the ink duplicating process is that when the master is fixed on the rotating drum of the duplicating machine (*e.g.* a Roneo or Gestetner duplicator), the ink is forced through the typewritten impressions, which have cut completely through the stencil, and a copy is produced on the duplicating paper when it comes in contact with the inked stencil. The typist should know how to cut the wax stencil which forms the master, and in order to cut a stencil which will produce good copies she should note carefully the following points:

(*a*) Choose a stencil sheet which is the correct size for the machine. The stencils have a backing sheet attached, which serves as a base upon which to type, and a thin sheet of carbon between the wax sheet and the backing sheet. The carbon provides a dark background so that the typist can more easily read what is typewritten, and it also produces a carbon copy on the backing sheet, which can be useful if the stencil is to be stored: when the stencil is inserted on the duplicating machine, the backing sheet and the carbon paper will be removed. The wax stencil itself is marked with horizontal and vertical lines, indicating the typewriting area for various sizes of paper. The typist must make sure that she does not type outside the lines appropriate to the size of paper she wishes to use for the copies.

(*b*) The typewriter must have typefaces which are clean and in good condition. The type must be cleaned with a stiff brush before and after every stencil is typed, and also during the actual typing if the work is lengthy.

(*c*) Insert the stencil in the typewriter, disengage the ribbon (using the "stencil" switch) and commence the typewriting, taking care to keep within the ruled frame. The touch must be very even, and the keys struck with a firm, staccato movement, so that the stencil is clearly cut. If an electric typewriter is being used, the touch switch may be adjusted and the typewriting will automatically be perfectly even, regardless of how hard the keys are struck. If the typefaces are fairly new (and therefore rather sharp), care must be taken with the typing of the letters "o" and "c," as a complete circle of stencil may be cut out if the keys are struck too hard.

(*d*) If a typewriting error occurs, correcting fluid (a clear, sticky liquid which hardens in the air), must be painted over the offending letter or word and left to dry for half a minute or so. When dry, the correct letter or word may be typed over the hardened liquid and, if it is done neatly, the error will not show on the final copy.

If a large portion (*e.g.* a whole paragraph), has been wrongly typed, it is possible completely to cover up the mistake by grafting on a piece of wax stencil cut from another sheet. The wrong portion is cut out of the stencil in use, and a new piece of stencil (which must be slightly larger than the piece which has been removed) is stuck over the space, with edges overlapping. Correcting fluid is used to stick the edges firmly and, when it is dry it can be typed on in the normal way.

(*e*) Thoroughly check the typewritten matter before the stencil is removed from the machine. The stencil is now ready to be put on to the duplicator.

(*f*) Stencils can also be cut by hand, using a stylus; this is often used for ruling long lines, drawing diagrams, the signature at the end of a circular letter, mathematical signs or ordinary handwriting.

(*g*) If multi-coloured copies are required, a separate stencil for each colour must be cut. The wording, etc., must be most carefully placed in the correct position on the sheet as, when running off the copies, a separate run is required for each colour, using different stencils for each run. The drum on the duplicator is changed each time, since each drum contains different coloured ink.

(*h*) After the copies have been run off, the stencil may be stored for further use, either by hanging in a special cabinet, or by being laid flat on its backing sheet in a suitable box or folder. If desired, the ink may be cleaned off with a special solution supplied by the manufacturers.

4. Spirit duplicating. Up to 300 copies may be produced on a spirit duplicator but, as with the ink duplicating process, a master is required. The master in this case is a sheet of art paper (shiny on one side) on which the wording will eventually appear in the negative; this can be obtained in several sizes.

The principle of the spirit duplicating process is that a special carbon paper (coated with an aniline dye and sometimes called a *hectographic transfer sheet*), is used to produce the negative impression on the master. The spirit in the duplicator reacts with the dye—in fact, the dye is soluble in the spirit, and the copying paper, which may be of any kind, comes into contact with the master after this reaction has begun. A positive (as opposed to a negative) copy, is made.

This method of duplicating can be used for many kinds of work, such as typewritten documents, handwriting, drawings, diagrams, etc., and the special carbon sheets can be obtained in several colours.

To prepare a master, the procedure is as follows:

(*a*) Take one special carbon sheet and one sheet of art paper, and place the shiny side of the art paper against the carbon-coated side of the carbon sheet. Insert them together into the typewriter, with the art paper facing uppermost when the platen is rolled into position.

(*b*) Commence typing directly on to the master in the normal manner (*i.e.* the ribbon need not be disengaged). The carbon will then be transferred in negative form, on to the back of the master at the position of the wording.

(*c*) If an error occurs, the carbon may be gently scraped off the back of the art paper with a razor blade or penknife, and the correct letter or word retyped over it. Alternatively, special correcting fluid may be used to remove the carbon from the master.

(*d*) When a different colour is required, it is necessary to remove the sheets from the typewriter, and re-insert the master with a different coloured carbon sheet.

(*e*) The masters may be prepared by hand, using any normal writing tool, *e.g.* pen, ball-point pen, pencil.

(*f*) The master can be stored flat, if required for further use, but it must be remembered that any one master will produce only about 300 good copies.

5. Offset lithography. The master for the offset litho process may be either a metal plate or a paper plate; up to 50,000 copies may be obtained from the former, and up to 2000 from the latter. The copies are of very high quality, and this process may be used for producing large quantities of any commercial document, *e.g.* circulars, price lists, etc., on any type or size of paper.

The principle of the offset litho process is that the writing on the master (or whatever is to be copied) is finally produced in a positive form on a plate, using a greasy substance.

When the master is put on to the roller of the machine, it is dampened with water, which is absorbed by the non-greasy parts and rejected by the greasy parts. The master then comes in contact with the ink, which adheres to the greasy parts and is rejected by the dampened parts. The image is then "offset" (negatively) on to a rubber roller which in turn, will produce a positive copy on the copying paper.

There are several ways of preparing the master, but the typist would usually be concerned only with typewriting or handwriting, since other methods involve electronic scanners or special copying processes, both normally dealt with by specially trained personnel.

To prepare a typewritten master:

(a) Fit the typewriter with a special litho ribbon.

(b) Insert the special litho plate into the typewriter, taking great care when handling it as there must be no greasy finger marks, dirty marks or smudges.

(c) Commence typing, using a normal, even touch; the pressure must not be so great as completely to cut through the plate, but sufficient to make an impression; after typing, the impressions should look even and clear.

(d) If an error occurs, the greasy impression may be removed with a special offset eraser, but the plate must not be damaged or scraped when erasing. The correct letter or word can then be retyped.

(e) The masters can be prepared by hand, using offset ink or special carbon paper.

(f) If several colours are required, a separate master must be prepared for each colour, since, as with the rotary ink duplicator, a separate run is necessary for each master, changing the ink each time.

6. Copying machines. Producing copies on a copying machine differs from the other methods of duplicating, inasmuch as no master is required, and the copies produced are exact replicas of the original document—corrections, signatures, marks, or anything else appearing on the original will appear on the copies.

XI. COPYING AND DUPLICATING 151

The principle of the copying process is that the original is photographed, and from the negative a positive copy is produced on the special copying paper. The actual photographic process may differ from one type of machine to another, but for producing only a few copies (six to eight), using a copying machine is economical, quick and easy.

PROGRESS TEST 11

1. List the different methods by which copies may be produced. Which methods would you use for the following purposes:

(a) Two copies of a short letter.
(b) Eight copies of a page from a book which includes a diagram.
(c) Ten thousand copies of a circular.
(d) Fifty copies of a notice for internal circulation.
(e) Two thousand copies of a notice to be sent through the post. (**1–6**)

2. What points must be remembered when:

(a) Handling and storing carbon paper.
(b) Typing carbon copies? (**2**)

3. How would you correct errors on the following:

(a) A carbon copy.
(b) A wax stencil.
(c) A hectograph carbon. (**2–4**)

4. What points must be remembered when cutting a wax stencil? (**3**)

5. How are multi-coloured copies produced on an ink duplicator? (**3**)

6. Describe the principle of the spirit duplicating process. (**4**)

7. How would you prepare a typewritten master for a spirit duplicating machine? (**4**)

8. How would you prepare a typewritten master for offset lithography? (**5**)

Type one copy of this application form, leaving appropriate spaces for the answer to each question.

APPLICATION FOR LOAN

1. Full name (Mr/Mrs/Miss):
   Date + place of birth:
   Address:

   Tel. No.:

2. Name of employer:
   Address:

   Nature of employment:
   Length of present employment:

3. Name and address of Banker:

4. Address of property (if not as in No. 1 above):

   State if freehold or leasehold:
   If mortgaged, give name + address of mortgagee:

   N.C. Give name of finance company for any current or recent credit transactions:
   Your reference No.:

5. Estimated cost of work:
   Name and address of contractor:

6. Amount of loan requested:
   Number of monthly repayments proposed:

   Signature _ _ _ _ _ _ _ _ _ Date _ _ _ _ _ _ _ _

   If under 2 years' residence, give previous address:

R.S.A.—INTERMEDIATE 1971

CHAPTER XII

SHORTHAND-TYPEWRITING AND AUDIO-TYPEWRITING

1. The shorthand-typist. The main duty of a shorthand-typist is to receive dictation and to transcribe her shorthand notes on the typewriter. The type of work will vary from one office to another, but will consist mainly of correspondence, with some notices, reports, memos, etc.

The qualities necessary in a good shorthand-typist are varied, but the most important are as follows:

(a) *An adequate shorthand speed.* The minimum speed necessary for most appointments is at least 100 words per minute.

(b) *Complete accuracy in writing shorthand.* This means, of course, that the shorthand writer must know the system really well. Employers want their letters transcribed exactly, when they have bothered to dictate them carefully, and do not expect the shorthand-typist to make guesses.

(c) *A good command of the English language.* Spelling and punctuation are especially important. The shorthand-typist must have a good dictionary in which she can check the spelling of words about which she is doubtful.

(d) *A reasonable typewriting speed.* A good knowledge of typewriting procedures and of the layout of various documents is also important. The minimum speed necessary is about fifty words per minute, but it must be remembered that this does not indicate the *transcription* speed. The transcription speed is considerably less, but, obviously, the more practice a person can get, the higher the speed obtained.

(e) *A good knowledge of general office duties.* The shorthand-typist may be asked to undertake other jobs in the office, such as cutting stencils, duplicating, filing or attending to the post.

2. Receiving dictation. The shorthand-typist must always have her notebook ready, with pen or pencil at hand. The notebook should have ready-ruled margins and plenty of empty pages, in case the dictating session is a long one. When receiving dictation:

(*a*) Pay attention to the sense of the matter, as this assists when transcribing.

(*b*) If a word is not clear, do not hesitate to ask the person giving the dictation, either at the time or, if not convenient then, at a suitable pause in the dictation. A ring can be placed around any word that is doubtful.

(*c*) If the dictation is too fast, say so. An employer would rather slow down a little than have an incorrect document placed before him.

(*d*) Punctuate the shorthand as much as possible when actually writing it—definitely insert all full stops, and indicate new paragraphs if possible—this is a great help when transcribing.

(*e*) Use the margin for additional notes, such as special instructions, or spellings of unusual names, and indicate any letters, etc., which are urgent and need to be typed first.

(*f*) Date the shorthand page at the beginning of each day's work; this might be useful at a later date if notes have to be referred to again.

(*g*) Always make sure that the addressee's correct name and address is received; this will either be in the dictation itself, or, more usually, the person dictating will hand the letter to which he is replying to the shorthand-typist after the dictation has been completed.

(*h*) Alterations and corrections must be dealt with neatly. A wide margin, and ample space left after the completion of each piece, are useful for entering any additions or alterations.

3. Transcribing shorthand notes. Transcription of shorthand notes should be done as soon as possible after receiving them. While it is true to say that a good shorthand note will be readable forever, it is probably speedier to transcribe it if the note is fresh in the mind. When transcribing:

XII. SHORTHAND-TYPEWRITING AND AUDIO-TYPEWRITING 155

(a) Always read the shorthand through completely before beginning to type, for the following reasons:

  (i) It reminds the typist of the topic.
  (ii) It conveys the sense of the piece more fully.
  (iii) It enables the typist to estimate the amount of paper required.
  (iv) It enables the typist to decide on a suitable style and layout for the whole piece.
  (v) It gives an opportunity to sort out any queries beforehand.
  (vi) It allows the typist to insert extra punctuation marks, and to mark paragraphs, indentations, etc.

(b) Assemble the necessary paper, carbons, etc., and commence typing. The urgent items should always be transcribed first.

(c) Try always to read your shorthand a few words ahead all the time, so that typewriting can continue smoothly and evenly throughout.

(d) Consult a dictionary if there is doubt about any spellings.

(e) The document must be checked very carefully, *before* removing the paper from the machine.

(f) Type the envelope, if necessary, and put it with the letter in the pile waiting for signatures. Urgent correspondence should be presented for signature as soon as possible, and must not be left in the pile until all the other work is completed.

4. Audio-typewriting. Audio-typewriting is often used instead of shorthand-typewriting, and the typist wishing to do this kind of work should be fully trained in the skill. The audio-typist should possess some of the qualities of a shorthand typist, especially those pertaining to a good command of the English language (**1** (c)), a reasonable typewriting speed (**1** (d)), and a good general knowledge of office duties (**1** (e)). The audio-typist should have the following additional qualities:

(a) A thorough understanding of the working of her particular dictating machine.

(b) Good hearing; she should not be irritated by the earphones.

(c) An ability to type easily and fluently when there is no copy to look at.

(d) An ability to retain words.

5. Transcribing recorded dictation.

(a) Some indication of the length of the letter will be given, and the typist should assemble the necessary paper, carbons, etc., beforehand.

(b) Read or listen to any special instructions regarding the layout or style, number of copies, etc.

(c) If the voice of the person speaking is unfamiliar, listen to at least the first few sentences of the dictation, before commencing to type.

(d) Note any corrections listed on the index slip provided.

(e) Try always to listen a few words ahead, in order to maintain the sense, and so that the proper punctuation and paragraphing can be inserted.

(f) Ideally, the dictation should continue smoothly, without any break, and at the appropriate speed. This is not always possible, and the typist might have periodically to stop the machine while she catches up; these breaks should be as few as possible.

(g) Any words not clearly audible should be checked with the person giving the dictation. A dictionary must be consulted for any spelling queries.

(h) Re-run the dictation, in order that the letter may be checked for possible omissions and typing errors.

(i) As with shorthand-typewriting, type the envelope if necessary, and complete urgent letters first.

6. Typing direct from dictation. To be able satisfactorily to type a document direct from dictation, *i.e.* typing at the same time as the employer is dictating, the typist must have an accurate typewriting speed of at least seventy words per minute. This method of dictating might be used in an emergency for a short letter or memo, but for a longer document it is not really economical from the point of view of the employer's time.

7. Other secretarial duties. An efficient shorthand- or audio-typist may be asked to perform some tasks which could be classed as personal secretarial duties. Such duties might include:

(*a*) Composing letters from brief notes.
(*b*) Compiling reports and summaries.
(*c*) Preparing itineraries.

A brief discussion of these topics appears below, but the reader is advised to obtain a copy of a good book describing secretarial practice in more detail, if she is interested in this aspect of office work.

(*a*) *Composing letters from brief notes.* The typist must be familiar with the construction of a business letter, as well as the styles of layout, etc. (*see* I and II).

When composing a business letter, the following points should be borne in mind:

  (*i*) The correct salutation and complimentary close must be used.
  (*ii*) The message must be clear, concise and without ambiguity.
  (*iii*) The construction must be simple and direct, avoiding outmoded phrases and involved sentences.
  (*iv*) The tone of the letter must be polite and courteous.
  (*v*) The letter should include a suitable opening sentence, followed by the body of the message, and a closing sentence.
  (*vi*) The body of the letter must be divided into suitable paragraphs, expressing the contents in a logical order, each paragraph leading naturally to the next.
  (*vii*) Great care must be taken with punctuation and spelling.

(*b*) *Compiling reports and summaries.* A report or summary may have to be made of a meeting, a conference, a discussion, or an existing state of affairs (*e.g.* the necessity or otherwise of obtaining some new office equipment). The typist should begin by drawing up a rough outline of the points to be stated, so that the essential facts will be logically arranged.

The finished document will consist of the following:

  (*i*) *The heading*, containing the subject, date, place (if applicable), with the names of people present (if it is a meeting), and the name of the person to whom the report or summary will be sent.
  (*ii*) *The opening paragraph*, which describes the circum-

stances making necessary the report or summary (if applicable).

(iii) *The body of the report*, which should present the facts in an accurate, clear and concise way; construction of sentences should be kept as simple as possible, giving no irrelevant details. A meeting or event is usually reported in the third person, in the past tense; an individual report (*e.g.* from a secretary to her employer) is reported in the first person. Sub-headings are generally used, especially when reporting a meeting.

(iv) *The closing paragraphs*, which contain any necessary recommendations, with suggestions for appropriate action (if applicable); the date and place of the next meeting should also be included, if relevant. The name of the author of the report, with the designation, is typed at the end. See III for details of the layout and typewriting of manuscript reports.

(c) *Preparing itineraries* (see Fig. 60). A good selection of the appropriate reference books is necessary to compile an itinerary (*see* XIV, **6**)

```
                        ITINERARY

                  MEETING  OF  DIRECTORS

                Tuesday, 14th January, 197-

      Depart       Bristol (Temple Meads)   07.30 hours
      Arrive       London (Paddington)      09.25 hours
                   (To be met by T. Smith, Esq.)
      Meeting at the Grand Hotel,
                       John Street, WIN 2HQ 10.00 hours
      Depart       London (Paddington)      18.40 hours
      Arrive       Bristol (Temple Meads)   20.40 hours


      Note: Breakfast is available on the morning train.
            Dinner is available on the evening train.
```

FIG. 60.—*An itinerary*

The information required for an itinerary includes the following:

- (*i*) Dates, places and times of arrival and departure of trains, planes or other methods of transport, with sleeping berth or cabin numbers.
- (*ii*) Details of hotel accommodation.
- (*iii*) Dates, places and times of meetings or conferences.
- (*iv*) Any other relevant information, such as whether the person is to be met at the station, or whether a meal is available on the train.

The itinerary is typed on a card about the size of a postcard and all items should be arranged neatly and clearly in chronological order. If the itinerary covers a long period a larger size of paper may be necessary.

PROGRESS TEST 12

1. What qualities should a good shorthand-typist possess? (**1**)

2. What advice would you give to a shorthand-typist about to receive her first dictation in the office? (**2**)

3. Why is it better to read a shorthand note through completely before commencing to transcribe? (**3**)

4. How should urgent correspondence be dealt with? (**3**)

5. List the points to be remembered when transcribing recorded dictation. (**5**)

6. What are the essentials of a good business letter? (**7**)

7. If your employer was going abroad on a business trip and asked you to prepare an itinerary, what information would he expect to find on it when completed? (**7**)

BUSINESS TYPEWRITING

Type the following letter to Mr. Jack Holden, The Lodge, Green Lane, Epsom, Surrey. Use plain A5 paper—cut or fold a piece of A4 paper to obtain this size; do *not* tear. Take one carbon copy on the flimsy yellow paper provided.

5 Queen's Terrace,
Crawley.
Sussex.
21.6.71

Dear Jack,

You will remember that when we met last wk. we were talking about the need for the "Concorde" in relation to the time taken in getting from the centre of cities to the airports. I thought you might, therefore, be interested in the enclosed information taken from a diagram wh. appeared in last Sunday's paper. Perhaps there is something in what you say, after all!

I was delighted to hear that Peter has passed his driving test at the first attempt. Please convey my congratulations to him.

Yours sincerely.

R.S.A.—ADVANCED 1971

CHAPTER XIII

TYPEWRITING TECHNIQUE

1. Qualities of a competent typist. A competent typist is one who can produce good typewritten work in a reasonable time. To be able to do this the typist should be:

(a) Familiar with all aspects of typewriting theory.

(b) Able to type by the "touch" method, *i.e.* not looking at the keyboard.

(c) Able to type neatly and accurately at a reasonable speed.

(d) In possession of a typewriter in good order.

(e) Able to work easily in an "office" atmosphere.

2. Common typewriting errors. Here are some of the most common errors made by typists, with hints on how they can be cured:

(a) *Lightly-typed letters.* Practise words containing the faulty letters frequently, with other words containing letters typed by the same "weak" finger.

(b) *Omission of letters or words.* Keep your eyes on the copy at all times and do not read ahead.

(c) *Raised capitals.* Practise shift-key exercises.

(d) *Uneven left-hand margins.* Practise returning the carriage with slightly more pressure. With a smooth-running machine, it should not be necessary to keep the hand on the carriage-return lever for the whole distance; if the fault persists, it may mean that the carriage needs oiling.

(e) *Transposed letters.* Do not read ahead in the copy, and slow down the typing speed.

(f) *Piling (or crowding) letters.* Type more evenly, and slow down the typing speed.

(g) *Clashing the typebars.* As for (f).

(h) *Omitting spaces.* As for (e).

(i) *Inserting extra spaces*. Practise "bouncing" the thumb off the space bar while typing short words from copy.

(j) *Wrong letters*. If errors frequently occur, try to analyse the mistakes to see if any are recurrent. If a particular letter is often wrongly typed practise as many words as possible containing that letter, using the appropriate drills from a typewriting manual.

(k) *Overtyping*. This is severely penalised in examinations. In the beginning, it is often due to laziness, but if frequently employed it can become a habit which is difficult to break. The typist must learn to stop and erase every time an error occurs.

NOTE: Many errors can be avoided if the typist adopts a good posture, concentrates on what she is doing, watches the copy, and practises frequently.

3. Correction of errors.

(a) *Typewriting rubber*. When erasing faulty letters, or words with a typewriting rubber, observe the following precedure:

    (i) Move the carriage to the left or to the right, so that any rubber dust will fall on to the desk and not into the type-basket.

    (ii) Turn up the platen so that the portion to be erased is resting on the metal plate over the roller. If the error occurs near the bottom of the page, it is best to turn the platen backwards, and so bring the portion to be erased up from the back of the machine on to the metal plate.

    (iii) Erase the letter, or word, neatly, taking care not to spoil the adjoining letters (an erasure shield may be used to protect the other letters). Lightly blow the rubber dust away from the typewriter and make sure the error is completely erased.

    (iv) Return the carriage and line of typing to the correct position, and type in the letter or word.

(b) *Chemicals*. When erasing with chemically treated or powder-covered strips of paper, observe the following precedure:

    (i) Back-space to the letter or word to be covered.

    (ii) Place the special strip of paper between the error and the typewriter ribbon.

(*iii*) Retype the same error (through the strip).
(*iv*) Remove the strip, back-space to the original position; retype the letter or word correctly.

Erasing with powder-covered strips of paper is not as permanent as erasing with a rubber, because when the papers are handled or rubbed together frequently, the powder may eventually rub off and the original error will be exposed.

(*c*) *Erasing liquid.* A liquid is available which can be painted over errors, and when it is dry the correct letter or word is typed in. The liquid is available in several colours, but as it takes a while to dry it is not necessarily quicker than erasing with a rubber.

(*d*) *Back-feeding.* It may be necessary to make a correction after the paper has been taken out of the machine. This would normally be done by inserting the paper back into the machine (after erasing the error), and aligning the point of typewriting by use of the paper-release lever and the variable line-spacer.

Sometimes, however, the papers may have been fastened together with a clip or ribbon, which makes it impossible to insert the paper in the machine in the usual way. In these cases, the papers are inserted into the machine from the front, which is called "back-feeding." To do this, observe the following procedure.

(*i*) Insert a loose sheet of paper into the machine in the normal way, rolling it on until about 1 in. is clear of the platen.
(*ii*) Insert the bottom of the page to be corrected into the front of the machine, placing it between the platen and the loose sheet of paper.
(*iii*) Roll the platen backwards until the main sheet of paper is firmly gripped, and the spare sheet comes out of the back (or it may be removed by using the paper-release lever).
(*iv*) Position the main sheet exactly, and retype the letter or word.

(*e*) *Half-space correcting.* This is used when a word, consisting of one letter more than the original word, has to be typed in the same amount of space as the original word occupied; or if a letter has been omitted, and you have, for example, to type four letters in the space normally occupied by three.

(i) Erase the original word neatly.
(ii) Position the typewriting point at the place where the first erased letter was typed.
(iii) Half-depress the back-space key (keeping the finger on the key); the carriage is now moved back half a space.
(iv) Type in the first letter of the group, and then release the back-spacer.
(v) Repeat (iii) and (iv) until all new letters are typed.

This procedure may be adapted if you have to insert a word consisting of one letter less than the original word.

(f) For correction of carbon copies and masters, *see* XI.

NOTE: Always check the work very carefully *before* removing the papers from the machine.

4. Care of the typewriter. A typewriter kept in good condition will, with a competent typist, always produce good work. The following points should be observed by the typist:

(a) Keep the typewriter clean. Use a stiff brush to clean the keys regularly, and a soft, long-handled brush to clean inside the machine. All rubber dust must be brushed away frequently, as it can clog the mechanism; it is especially important to clean the type well after typing on a wax stencil.

(b) Clean the bodywork and platen with a soft duster and methylated spirit (supplied by a typewriter shop or any chemist).

(c) Keep the machine covered when it is not in use.

(d) When lifting the machine, lock the carriage (by placing both margin stops in the centre), and hold it so that the keys are facing away from the body. This places the greatest weight high up your arms, and there is less chance of the machine being dropped.

(e) Lightly oil the carriage runners from time to time. Do not oil heavily, and always use special typewriter oil. Leave internal oiling to the typewriter mechanic.

(f) Have the machine serviced regularly by a reputable dealer.

(g) If the machine goes wrong, call the mechanic, unless the fault is obvious and can easily be put right by the typist. Never try to probe inside the machine.

(h) Keep the machine away from excessive heat, or the ribbon will dry up.

(i) Replace the ribbon when necessary, not only because otherwise the typing will be faint, but also because the typeface will cut into the roller if the ribbon is very worn.

(j) Always use a backing sheet when typing. This prolongs the life of the roller and produces better typewritten copy.

PROGRESS TEST 13

1. List the typewriting errors that most frequently occur. How can these errors be avoided? (**2**)

2. Describe two methods of correcting errors in typewritten copy. What do you understand by the following terms:

(a) Back-feeding.

(b) Half-space correcting? (**3**)

3. How would a typist keep her typewriter in good condition? (**4**)

Type one copy of the following on plain white paper.
No carbon copy is required.

BANKING SERVICES

The following are some of the services provided by the banks:-

3. The cheque system - by use of a current a/c - an easy & safe method of payment of bills, etc.
6. Gift cheques
9. The issue of foreign currency & traveller's cheques
8. The provision of drafts, letter payments, & telegraphic transfers for foreign payments which
1. Facilities to deposit money ~~which~~ will earn interest (a deposit account) (trading conditions abroad)
12. The ability to supply information re markets &
2. The loan of money to approved borrowers (by means of bank loans & bank overdrafts)
4. Standing orders - the bank monthly makes regular payments of bills for customers, eg., mortgage payments, insurance premiums, annual subscriptions
5. Transfer of credit - by means of a credit card transfer or credit card system
7. The discounting of Bills of Exchange
10. Action as executor and/or trustee
11. The provision of comprehensive banking facilities

(A leaflet attached - see also the books in the Office Appliance Centre - for expansion on this. Homework can be set from any of the questions at the end of the chapter in the students' textbook.) (for those engaged in oversea trade)

ACCOUNTING/DISCOUNTING

TYPIST
Rearrange in numerical order retaining the numbers. You may use either 'hanging' or 'block' style.

R.S.A.—ELEMENTARY 1971

XIII. TYPEWRITING TECHNIQUE

On the headed A.4 paper, type the following letter for despatch today, taking one carbon copy on yellow paper.

Mr. F. Jamieson,
10 Ashdown Street, EDINBURGH. EH2 4QX

Dear Mr. Jamieson,

I should like your comments on the following passage, which I suggest should replace the article at present printed on page viii of our catalogue.

PEACHES AND NECTARINES

INDENT FROM MARGIN →

The peach is very similar to the nectarine but has a downy instead of a smooth skin. Like the pear both are among the juiciest of the larger fruits, but are not so hardy as smaller fruits such as the plum & cherry. Nowadays the tendency is to grow them under cover & protect them from so various diseases which attack them — cold Spring winds check the sap & cause a disease called "blister"; they attract

l.c./

N.P./

black fly and are quite susceptible to mildew. [Peaches may be planted from Nov. to March in the open, but against the shelter of a wall. It is best to start with a 3-year-old tree and prune the branches during the first & second years, to produce a good woody lower part of the tree which will give off young fruiting side shoots. [Peaches & nectarines are sometimes grown under a lean-to. It is possible for older trees to give fruit in June if they have been planted towards the end of ~~December~~. Peaches soon suffer from dryness either in the soil or in the atmosphere. To commence with, the temperature should be low — a night temperature of 45°F and a day temperature of 55°F, but, as the fruit grows, another 10° may be given. From March the sun will soon add to the temperature & ventilation must be increased.

N.P./
(the roof of)

stet/

It is intended eventually to re-write all the descriptive articles in the catalogue and I should be glad to receive from you any recommendations for the new wording.

, so the glasshouse should be syringed daily

Yours sincerely,

R.S.A.—ELEMENTARY 1971

CHAPTER XIV

REFERENCE BOOKS

1. The need for reference books. Every typist, shorthand-typist and private secretary should have access to a comprehensive selection of reference books. Not all the books described below are essential for every office worker, but a good pocket English dictionary should be in every typist's desk drawer; books such as the telephone directory or the *Post Office Guide* should be available when needed.

The typist must make herself familiar with these reference books, know the scope of their contents and how to use them, and she should practise looking up information in a quick and efficient manner.

2. Reference books on English.

(*a*) *English dictionary.* There are several good English dictionaries, but the *Concise Oxford Dictionary* can be particularly recommended.

(*b*) *Fowler's Modern English Usage.* This explains points of grammar and the general usage of the English language.

(*c*) *Roget's Thesaurus of English Words and Phrases.* This is different from a dictionary, inasmuch as the words are arranged in groups according to their meaning, and not in alphabetical order. It is used for finding synonyms and antonyms, and gives all the "shades" of meaning a simple phrase or a single word can have. For example, another word meaning the same as "twinkle" might be required. Look up "twinkle" in the index. Against it are several numbers each referring to a paragraph in the main text dealing with a different meaning of "twinkle." If you wanted another word for the "light" meaning of "twinkle," look at this particular paragraph, and you will find several possible alternatives, including "shine," "glow," "glitter," "glimmer" and "sparkle."

(*d*) *Dictionary of synonyms and antonyms.* This may be

XIV. REFERENCE BOOKS

used instead of (c), and the words here are arranged alphabetically.

3. Telephone directories. The local telephone directory, listing alphabetically the names, addresses and telephone numbers of telephone subscribers in the area, should always be available, and directories for other regions of the country can be obtained from the Post Office. These directories also contain "yellow pages" which list the names, addresses and telephone numbers of local tradesmen and professional people, under the heading of their trades and professions.

Telephone directories can be useful to the filing clerk or the typist who cannot remember the rules for listing items in alphabetical order—consulting a telephone directory would give a lot of help here.

4. Street directories. Directories, like *Kelly's Directory* or *the Post Office Directory*, first list names of streets of a particular area in alphabetical order, with the names of all occupiers of property in that street. Then the names of all residents in the area are listed alphabetically, with their addresses; trades and professions are also listed.

5. Post Office Guide. This gives detailed information relating to all the services of the Post Office. It is published annually and may be purchased from any Post Office; supplements are issued as necessary and are available on request. Listed in the Guide are such items as postal charges, maximum weights and sizes allowed for parcels, registration details, telephone service information, telegram charges, overseas postal rates, helpful advice on methods of packaging articles, National Savings and Giro information, and much more besides.

6. Travel information. There are numerous publications to help the traveller, the most common of which are as follows:

(a) *Ordnance Survey Maps.*

(b) *Timetables.* British Rail, the airline companies, coach and bus companies, and shipping lines all issue their own timetables. These give details of routes, times of trains, planes, coaches, buses, or boats, names of stopping places, with the times of arrival, and details of where to change trains, etc.

(c) *ABC Guides.* There are several issues of these, each dealing with a different mode of travel, *e.g. ABC Railway Guide, ABC Coach and Bus Guide, ABC Shipping Guide, ABC World Airways Guide.*

The Guides are similar to ordinary timetables, except that they show only the departure and arrival times at specific towns, cities and countries in an alphabetical list. Stops en route are not shown, neither are any changes which have to be made. Details of fares are included, with some information about the various places listed (*e.g.* population, distance from London, early closing days).

(d) *Handbooks of the Automobile Association and the Royal Automobile Club.* These are available only to members of the respective associations, and give information on road travel, approved garages and hotels and brief information on the places listed. Both associations also issue more specialised publications, such as the *Camping and Caravanning Handbook, Travelling Abroad*, etc., and they will also send itineraries and recommended routes on request.

(e) *Other travel books.* These include *Hotels in Great Britain and Northern Ireland* and *Lloyd's Shipping List* (published daily, giving movements of shipping).

7. Forms of Address.
The chief reference books giving this information are as follows:

(a) *Black's Titles and Forms of Address.*

(b) *Debrett's Peerage and Titles of Courtesy.*

(c) *Who's Who.* Which has many specialised editions, such as *Who's Who in the Theatre, The Catholic Who's Who, Who Was Who, International Who's Who, Who's Who in America*, etc.

(d) *Kelly's Handbook to the Titled Landed and Official Classes.*

(e) *Burke's Genealogical and Heraldic History of the Landed Gentry.*

(f) A *Typist's Desk Book.*

(g) A *Dictionary of Typewriting.*

8. Dictionaries.
Apart from an English dictionary, there may be others necessary to the typist, such as a shorthand

XIV. REFERENCE BOOKS

dictionary, a dictionary of quotations, a medical dictionary, a typewriting dictionary or a dictionary of legal terms. There are also many other specialised dictionaries which a particular firm might need.

9. Other reference books.

(a) *General Information*
  (i) Encyclopaedias. Some popular ones include *Encyclopaedia Britannica*, *Pears Cyclopaedia* and *Chamber's Encyclopaedia*.
  (ii) *Whitaker's Almanack*. A comprehensive reference book published annually, giving information on a wide variety of subjects, such as governments, the Royal Family, countries of the world, statistical information about population, etc. and weights and measures, and items on the significant drama, films and broadcasting of the year covered.

(b) *Trade Directories*:
  (i) Kelly's *Directory of Merchants, Manufacturers and Shippers*.
  (ii) *C.B.I. Register of British Manufacturers*.
  (iii) *Specialist trade directories*.

(c) *Legal reference books*.
  (i) Osborn's *Concise Law Dictionary*.
  (ii) *The Law List*. This gives details of legal personnel.
  (iii) Stone's *Justices' Manual*.

(d) *Political information*.
  (i) *Hansard*. This is issued daily, and is a verbatim record of the previous day's activities in both Houses of Parliament.
  (ii) A *Municipal Year Book*. This contains information about specific local authorities.
  (iii) *The Statesman's Year Book*. This contains information about the various governments of the world.

(e) *The Services*. The Army, Navy and Air Force all publish lists giving details of their officers, regiments, etc.

(f) *The Church*. Crockford's *Clerical Directory* gives details of Church of England clergy, and other denominations also publish details of their officials and activities.

(g) *Geographical information*.
  (i) Any good atlas, *e.g. The Times Atlas of the World*.
  (ii) Gazetteers. These give information about the impor-

tant cities and towns of the world. One in common use is Chamber's *World Gazetteer and Geographical Dictionary*.

(*h*) *Financial information.*
  (*i*) *The Financial Times.* This is published daily, and gives information on stocks and shares, etc.
  (*ii*) *The Stock Exchange Official Year Book.* This gives information on securities and investments, companies, etc.
  (*iii*) *Directory of Directors.* This lists the directors and officials of many companies.
  (*iv*) *Year Books.* These are published by financial institutions such as banks, insurance companies and building societies.

(*i*) *The Press and journalism.* Several publications are helpful here.
  (*i*) Willing's *Press Guide*.
  (*ii*) The *Newspaper Press Directory*.
  (*iii*) Publishing and press trade journals.

(*j*) *A Ready Reckoner.*

(*k*) *The Good Food Guide.* This lists hotels and restaurants with indications of price and various "star" ratings.

(*l*) *Trade journals.* These are published for numerous trades, giving up-to-date information and reports about their business.

PROGRESS TEST 14

1. (*a*) Which reference books do you consider to be essential to a typist? (**2–9**)

(*b*) Which reference books do you consider to be helpful but not essential to a typist? (**2–9**)

2. What information can be found in a telephone directory, apart from telephone numbers? (**3**)

3. Do you think the *Post Office Guide* is an essential reference book in the mail room of a large business concern? Give reasons for your answer. (**5**)

4. List the various reference books concerned with all types of travel. When might you use these books? (**6**)

5. What information is to be found in the following reference books:
  (*a*) *Roget's Thesaurus.*
  (*b*) *Whitaker's Almanack.*
  (*c*) *The AA Handbook.*
  (*d*) *The Law List.*
  (*e*) *Hansard.*
  (*f*) *The Good Food Guide.* (**2, 6, 9**)

XIV. REFERENCE BOOKS

Type one copy of the following on plain white paper.
No carbon copy is required.

Sources of Information & Reference *(Centre in Caps, Closed heart)*

The following reference books indicate comprehensive general information on quite a variety of subjects -

ENCYCLOPAEDIA BRITANNICA   PEARS CYCLOPAEDIA
CHAMBERS' ENCYCLOPAEDIA
WHITAKER'S ALMANACK

Information about prominent people can *(reference)* be referred to in the following books -

WHO'S WHO   DEBRETT'S PEERAGE   DIRECTORY OF DIRECTORS
CROCKFORD'S CLERICAL DIRECTORY   MEDICAL DIRECTORY
DENTISTS' REGISTER   REGISTER OF NURSES
NAVY, ARMY & AIR FORCE LISTS   REGISTERS OF PROFESSIONAL ASSOCIATIONS

(in any office) The following are useful for information about places and accommodation -

ANY ATLAS   KELLY'S DIRECTORIES   A to Z STREET GUIDES
AA & RAC HANDBOOKS   RAILWAY, COACH, BUS, SHIPPING & AIR GUIDES & TIMETABLES
HOTELS & RESTAURANTS IN BRITAIN

These books would be useful as sources of information about words and the English language -

THE SHORTER OXFORD *(DICTIONARY)* *(ENGLISH)*
THE CONCISE OXFORD DICTIONARY
A DICT. OF ABBREVIATIONS   PITMAN'S ENGLISH/SHORTHAND
THE " " TYPEWRITING   DICTIONARY
FOWLER'S MODERN ENGLISH USAGE

I think this will be sufficient without any further reference books being mentioned. Perhaps these can be learnt in the students' next private study period.

TYPIST - I would like each of the 5 paras. indented please, as shown. Each set of reference books should be typed in one column under the appropriate para. Please list them in the order indicated but do NOT type the numbers. I have written the names of the books in caps. — You can type them in l.c. or u.c. so long as you are consistent.

R.S.A.—INTERMEDIATE 1971

APPENDIX I

ABBREVIATIONS

1. General and manuscript abbreviations.

Abbreviation	*Meaning*
Abt.	about
A/c	account
advts. *or* adverts.	advertisements
aft.	after *or* afternoon
agn.	again
agst.	against
agt.	agent
altho.	although
amt.	amount
anon.	anonymous
ans.	answer
appro.	approval
approx.	approximate
arr.	arrive
art.	article
Assn.	Association
asst.	assistant
avge.	average
Bd.	Board
bk.	bank *or* book
bldg.	building
bn.	been
Br.	British
bro.	brother
Bt.	bought *or* Baronet
btwn.	between
cap.	capital
Capt.	Captain
cd.	could
ch. *or* chap.	chapter

Abbreviation	*Meaning*
Chrmn.	Chairman
circs.	circumstances
c/o	care of
Col.	Colonel
comee.	committee
confce.	conference
considn.	consideration
considrbl.	considerable
dept.	department
diff.	difference
diffclt.	difficult
diffrnt.	different
diffy.	difficulty
dist.	district
div.	division *or* dividend
Dr.	Doctor *or* debtor
dy.	delivery
E.	east
ea.	each
Ed.	Editor
edn.	edition
Eng.	England
entd.	entered
equ.	equal *or* equivalent
esp.	especially
estab.	establish
evng.	evening
evry.	every
evryth.	everything
exam.	examination
excdgly.	exceedingly

Abbreviation	Meaning	Abbreviation	Meaning
exch.	exchange	indpt.	independent
f.	for	inspr.	inspector
fac.	facsimile	internat.	international
favrbl.	favourable	lbl.	liberal
fcp.	foolscap	lbr.	labour
fgn.	foreign	Ld.	Lord
fig.	figure	ldr.	leader
fm.	from	Ldship.	Lordship
fol.	folio	Lieut.	Lieutenant
Fr.	French *or* franc *or* Father	Ltd.	Limited
		mag.	magazine
		max.	maximum
freqt.	frequent	min.	minimum
freqtly.	frequently	misc.	miscellaneous
ft.	feet *or* foot	mkt.	market
		mng.	morning *or* meaning
fur.	furlong		
fwd.	forward	mo.	month
gal.	gallon	mos.	months
G.B.	Great Britain	MS.	manuscript
gen.	general	MSS.	manuscripts
genly.	generally	mt.	might
gent.	gentleman	mtg.	meeting
gents.	gentlemen	mtr.	matter
Gov.	Government	N.	north
G.P.O.	General Post Office	nec.	necessary
		no.	number
gt.	great	nom.	nominal
h.	have	nos.	numbers
hcap.	handicap	notwstg.	notwithstanding
hd.	had	nr.	near
Hon.	honorary *or* honourable	ntheless.	nevertheless
		o.	of
h.p.	horse-power	objn.	objection
hr.	hour	o'c	o'clock
hun.	hundred	offl.	official
hvg.	having	opn.	opinion
immed.	immediate	oppy.	opportunity
immedly.	immediately	ord.	ordinary
imprv.	improve	othr.	other
impt.	important	%	per cent
imptce.	importance	p.	per *or* page
in.	inch *or* inches		
inc.	incorporate	P.O.	Post Office

Abbreviation	Meaning	Abbreviation	Meaning
para.	paragraph *or* begin new paragraph	sh.	shall
		shd.	should
		Soc.	Society
Parl.	Parliament	sp.	special
partic.	particular	St.	street *or* Saint
perfmce.	performance		
pp.	pages	std.	standard
pr.	pair	t.	that
praps.	perhaps	/	the
prefce.	preference	temp.	temporary
prefd.	preferred	tho.	though
prelimy.	preliminary	thr.	there or their
Pres.	President	thrfr.	therefore
Prof.	Professor	thro.	through
propr.	proprietor	thsd.	thousand
qlty.	quality	tht.	thought
ques. *or* qu.	question	tog.	together
		Treas.	Treasurer
qto.	quarto	U.K.	United Kingdom
qy.	query	univ.	university
ref.	reference	v.	very
regd.	registered	voly.	voluntary
rly.	railway	W.	west
rm.	ream *or* room	w.	with
S.	south	wd.	would
satisfn.	satisfaction	wh.	which
satisfty.	satisfactory	wk.	week
sd.	said	wkg.	working
sec.	secretary *or* section	wl.	will
		wr.	were
secd.	second	ws.	was
sev.	several	yest.	yesterday
sgd.	signed	yr.	your *or* year
Sgt.	Sergeant		

2. Business and technical abbreviations.

Abbreviation	Meaning	Abbreviation	Meaning
ad. val.	according to value	B.R.S.	British Road Services
A.O.B.	any other business		
b/d	brought down	B/S	Bill of Sale
B/E	Bill of Exchange	bal.	balance
b/f	brought forward	Bros.	brothers
B/L	Bill of Lading	bsh.	bushel

Abbreviation	Meaning	Abbreviation	Meaning
B.T.U.	British Thermal Unit	f.a.s.	free alongside, or free alongside ship
C.B.D.	Cash before delivery	F.a.q.	Fair average quality
c/d	carried down	f.i.t.	free of income tax
C. & F.	Cost and freight	f.o.b.	free on board
c/f	carried forward	f.o.r.	free on rail
C.i.f.	Cost, insurance and freight	f.o.t.	free on trucks
		fwd.	forward
C.i.f. & c.	Cost, insurance, freight and commission	G.M.T.	Greenwich Mean Time
		G.P.O.	General Post Office
C.i.f.c. & i.	Cost, insurance, freight, commission and insurance	g.	gramme
		gr.	gross
		gr. wt.	gross weight
cks.	casks	I.O.U.	I owe you
cm	centimetre	I.R.O.	Inland Revenue Office
C.O.D.	Cash on delivery		
Corpn.	Corporation	kg	kilogramme
Coy. or Co.	Company	km	kilometre
		m	metre or mile or minute
C/R	Company's risk		
Cr.	creditor	mg	milligramme
ctge.	cartage	mm	millimetre
C.W.O.	Cash with order	M.O.	Money order
cum. div.	with dividend	O. & M.	Organisation and methods
deg.	degree		
dft.	draft	o/c	overcharge
D/O	Delivery order	O.R.	Operational research
D/W	Dock warrant	o/s	outstanding
°C	degrees Centigrade	oz	ounce
°F	degrees Fahrenheit	p.a.	per annum
E.C.G.D.	Export Credits Guarantee Department	P.A.	Personal Assistant
		P.A.Y.E.	Pay As You Earn
		pd.	paid
		pkg.	package
E.E.	Errors excepted	P/N	Promissory note
E. & O.E.	Errors and omissions excepted	P.O.	Post Office or Postal Order
		pd	paid
E.T.A.	Estimated time of arrival	pr.	pair
		P.R.	Public Relations
E.T.D.	Estimated time of departure	p.w.	per week
		qnty.	quantity
exd.	examined	qr.	quarter

Abbreviation	Meaning	Abbreviation	Meaning
qt.	quart	sq.	square
recd.	received	S.S. *or* S/S	Steamship
rect.	receipt		
ref.	reference	std.	standard
reg. *or* regd.	registered	S.T.D.	Subscriber Trunk Dialling
rm.	ream	Stg.	Sterling
Ry.	Railway	T.	Tons
s.a.e.	stamped addressed envelope	u/c	undercharge
		vol.	volume
sh.	share	w/o	write off *or* written off
shipt.	shipment		
sk.	sack	wt.	weight
S/N	Shipping note	W/W	Warehouse warrant
S.O.	Seller's option	yd.	yard

3. Legal abbreviations

Abbreviation	Meaning	Abbreviation	Meaning
abstt.	abstract	co. claim	counter claim
acct.	accountant	col.	counsel
admix.	administratrix	commr.	Commissioner
admor.	administrator	compenson.	compensation
afft.	affidavit	concerng.	concerning
afsd.	aforesaid	convce.	conveyance
agrt.	agreement	contt.	contract
alteron.	alteration	co. pt.	counterpart
amendt.	amendment	deced.	deceased
anny.	annuity	declon.	declaration
applon.	application	defce.	defence
apptd.	appointed	deft.	defendant
arrangt.	arrangement	deld.	delivered
assns.	assigns	deposn.	deposition
attestn.	attestation	descdt.	descendant
ats.	at suit of	dischge.	discharge
atty.	attorney	doct.	document
authy.	authority	drs.	debtors
bef.	before	dwg. ho.	dwelling house
bequed.	bequeathed	easmt.	easement
bf.	brief	este.	estate
bkcy.	bankruptcy	evce.	evidence
chge.	charge	exors.	executors
co.	copy	f. co.	fair copy
codl.	codicil	freehd.	freehold

APPENDIX I

Abbreviation	Meaning
howr.	however
hrar.	hereafter
hrnar.	hereinafter
hrs.	heirs
htofore.	heretofore
incumbs.	incumbrances
indemy.	indemnity
indre.	indenture
inhance.	inheritance
instrons.	instructions
JJ.	Justices
judgt.	judgment
judre.	judicature
jurisdon.	jurisdiction
le.	lease
liquon.	liquidation
L.S.	Locus sigilli (place of the seal)
mentd.	mentioned
mtge.	mortgage
mtgee.	mortgagee
mtgor.	mortgagor
necy.	necessary
parcht.	parchment
parlars. *or* partics.	particulars
pchsr.	purchaser
pcl.	parcel
posson.	possession
ppse.	purpose
premes.	premises
prosecon.	prosecution
provo.	proviso
provons.	provisions
purst.	pursuant
Q.B.	Queen's Bench
Q.C.	Queen's Counsel
redemon.	redemption
reg.	regulation
remr.	remainder
reqd.	required

Abbreviation	Meaning
requns.	requisitions
residy.	residuary
respt.	respondent
revocon.	revocation
revon.	reversion
secy.	security
settlt.	settlement
signe.	signature
spa.	subpoena
statt.	statement
stp.	stamp
subseqtly.	subsequently
substtd.	substituted
succon.	succession
sums. *or* sus.	summons
survor.	survivor
tenemt.	tenement
testor.	testator
testrix.	testatrix
testt.	testament
tfer.	transfer
thabts.	thereabouts
thby.	thereby
thfm.	therefrom
thof.	thereof
thon.	thereon
thrin.	therein
thto.	thereto
tree.	trustee
v.	versus
valuon.	valuation
vors.	vendors
whas.	whereas
whatsr.	whatsoever
whby.	whereby
whof.	whereof
whr.	whether
whrin.	wherein
witht.	without
witned.	witnessed
witneth.	witnesseth

APPENDIX II

FORMS OF ADDRESS

Title	Form of Address	Salutation	Complimentary Close
Archbishop	His Grace the Lord Archbishop of ...	My Lord Archbishop	I have the honour to be, My Lord Archbishop, Your Lordship's obedient servant,
Baron	The Right Hon. Lord ...	My Lord	I am, My Lord, Your obedient servant,
Baroness	The Right Hon. Lady ...	Madam	I am, Madam, Your obedient servant,
Baronet	Sir ..., Bt.,	Sir	I am, Sir, Your obedient servant,
Baronet's wife	Lady ...	Madam	I am, Madam, Your obedient servant,
Bishop (with seat in Lords)	The Right Rev. the Lord Bishop of ...	My Lord Bishop	I have the honour to be, My Lord, Your obedient servant,
Bishop (not in Lords)	The Right Rev. the Bishop of ...	Sir	I am, Sir, Your obedient servant,
Clergyman	The Rev. ...	Reverend Sir	I am, Reverend Sir, Your obedient servant,
Countess	The Right Hon. The Countess of ...	Madam	I am, Madam, Your obedient servant,

APPENDIX II

Title	Form of Address	Salutation	Complimentary Close
Duchess	Her Grace the Duchess of . . .	Madam	I am, Madam, Your obedient servant,
Duke	His Grace the Duke of . . .	My Lord Duke	I remain, My Lord Duke, Your obedient servant,
Earl	The Right Hon. The Earl of . . .	My Lord	I am, My Lord, Your obedient servant,
Judge	The Hon. Mr. Justice . . .	Sir	I am, Sir, Your obedient servant,
The King	His Majesty the King	Sir (Your Majesty, in body of letter)	I have the honour to be, Sir, Your Majesty's obedient subject,
Knight	Sir . . .	Sir	I am, Sir, Your obedient servant,
Knight's wife	Lady . . .	Madam	I am, Madam, Your obedient servant,
Lord Mayor	The Lord Mayor of . . .	My Lord Mayor	I am, My Lord Mayor, Your obedient servant,
Lord Mayor's wife	The Lady Mayoress of . . .	My Lady Mayoress	I am, My Lady Mayoress, Your obedient servant,
Lord Provost	The Lord Provost of . . .	My Lord Provost	I am, My Lord Provost, Your obedient servant,
Mayor	The Worshipful Mayor of . . .	Sir	I am, Sir, Your obedient servant,
Mayor's wife	The Mayoress of . . .	Madam	I am, Madam, Your obedient servant,
Marchioness	The Most Hon. The Marchioness of . . .	Madam	I am, Madam, Your obedient servant,

Title	Form of Address	Salutation	Complimentary Close
Marquess	The Most Hon. The Marquess of	My Lord	I am, My Lord, Your obedient servant,
Prince	His Royal Highness the Prince of	Sir	I have the honour to be, Sir, Your Royal Highness's obedient servant,
Princess	Her Royal Highness Princess ...	Madam	I have the honour to be, Madam, Your Royal Highness's obedient servant,
Privy Councillor	The Right Hon. ...., P.C.,	Sir	I am, Sir, Your obedient servant,
The Queen	Her Majesty the Queen	Madam (Your Majesty, in body of letter)	I have the honour to be, Madam, Your Majesty's obedient subject,
Viscount	The Right Hon. the Viscount ...	My Lord	I am, My Lord, Your obedient servant,
Viscountess	The Right Hon. the Viscountess ...	Madam	I am, Madam, Your obedient servant,

APPENDIX III

EXAMINATION TECHNIQUE

1. Preparations. Careful and thorough preparation is essential for success, and the candidate should be familiar with all aspects of the examination. Any practical examination can seem formidable, but good preparation and the right frame of mind can do much to alleviate nervousness, and will help the candiate to feel more confident. When preparing for a typewriting examination:

(*a*) Obtain the syllabus and make sure all topics have been covered. The typist must be competent in all sections of that particular examination.

(*b*) Practise with as many past examination papers as possible. Take care with the time factor and aim always to complete the papers in the specified time. When practising a complete paper, estimate the approximate time allowed for each question, and try not to exceed that time; five or ten minutes must be allowed for reading through the questions and checking the work. Always aim at perfect accuracy.

(*c*) Revise all layouts and theory well beforehand.

(*d*) Ensure that the machine being used is in good order. If it is a strange machine, try to obtain permission to practise on it a few days before the actual examination, and again for half an hour before the time.

(*e*) Make sure that all the necessary pens, etc., are available. The things you must take to a typewriting examination include the following:

(*i*) Admission card.

(*ii*) One or two pencils.

(*iii*) Pen and black ink (or ball-point pen).

(*iv*) Pen and red ink (or ball-point pen).

(*v*) One-foot ruler (transparent is best).

(*vi*) Blotting paper.

(*vii*) Spare paper for rough notes or plans.

(*viii*) Typewriting rubber, and, if it is normally used, an erasure shield.

(*ix*) A4- and A5-size carbon paper (although this is usually provided by the examination centre).

(x) Some examining bodies do not supply the typewriting paper. The candidate should find out this beforehand, and bring plenty of paper if necessary.

(f) The candidate should not wear "best" clothes for an examination. Everyday clothes are more familiar and, therefore, probably more relaxing.

2. Taking the examination. The candidate should arrive at the centre at least twenty minutes before the time of the examination. During this time she will be able to compose herself, and she will then be required to fill up the front page of the covers (in which the finished papers will eventually be put), with her name, address and other details—these are written in pen and ink. On the outside of the cover will be printed a number—this number must be typed on every sheet of paper used in the examination; no other identification is necessary. The covers will contain plain and headed typewriting paper of various sizes, on which the answers will be typed.

On receiving the question paper, the candidate should proceed as follows:

(a) Look at it very carefully and make sure you have thoroughly read and understand the instructions on the front page.

(b) Begin the first question (which is usually a warming-up copying test) and although few marks are awarded for it, it should be typed as accurately as possible. No more than about five minutes should be spent on this question.

(c) Read through the rest of the paper, and estimate the time required for each question. Jot down these times, and stick to them as far as possible.

(d) Complete the rest of the paper, taking great care to follow any instructions. Work calmly through each question—do not rush or panic. If a question is badly done, do not attempt to retype it immediately, as this may not leave sufficient time to complete the paper; continue until all questions are finished and then retype the incorrect question if there is any available time. Check every page for errors, before it comes out of the machine.

(e) On completion, check that each question has been attempted, and that the number is typed on every sheet. Sort the papers into order, beginning with the first question. Incorrect sheets of any questions which have been retyped should have a bold cross written through them, and these, with any spare blank sheets, are put at the end of the pile. All sheets and rough paper should be inserted in the covers provided and handed to the invigilator. Make sure that nothing is left on the desk.

(*f*) If the typewriter should prove faulty during an examination, the candidate must inform the invigilator, who will make a note of it in the space provided on the outer cover.

APPENDIX IV

EXAMINATION PAPERS

On the form provided, type the following memorandum, for dispatch today, from the General Manager to the Personnel Manager. Take one carbon copy on white paper.

SUBJECT: Pension/Life Assurance   /Caps.

I have decided that my office shall keep a record of all applications for entry into the Pension/Life Assurance Scheme and I should be glad if you would have a form printed which will provide the necessary details. I enclose a suggested draft of the form, 1,000 of which should be printed in the first instance.

(Please let me see a proof as soon as possible.)

Typist:

Please type the following note at the top of the carbon copy:—

Mr. Jones: Please bring forward on 7th December.

R.S.A.—ELEMENTARY 1970

APPENDIX IV

The following is to be typed on headed paper and addressed to Mr. E. Turner, White Gates, East Common, Huntingdon—today's date—one carbon copy on yellow paper.

Dear Mr. Turner,

With reference to our conversation last week, I have found out some more information regarding the pneumatic fork (brick). The fork is adaptable to any shape or size of Brick. The standard model with 235 mm tine spacing adapts to any brick between 57 and 146 mm wide. It comes with 5 to 10 tines to fit all sizes of Truck. A bigger one will carry up to 1,000 green Bricks and up to 1,500 fired bricks.

The spacings of the tines can be also modified to enable them to be used for both metric and imperial bricks, which is most important during the period of changeover to the metric system.

A smaller one will carry 500 green bricks and about 750 fired bricks.

The fork can be used for the new type of SHRINK FILM PACKAGING and can be adapted to pick up a package which has been built with appropriate holes through it to accept specially large tines. A package which has been supported on a pallet or

The fork is at present in the prototype stage but it is anticipated that when it gets into quantity production, the price will not be greater than $55 (this includes the alternative types of tines for different types of packages).

I hope you will have a most successful trip to Australia next month.

Yours sincerely,

Chief Accountant.

R.S.A.—INTERMEDIATE 1970

Type one copy of the following price-list. Put the items in numerical order but do not insert the numbers.

HARD FRUIT BUSHES (Spaced caps.)

WILL GROW IN ANY REASONABLE SOIL } (Closed caps.)
PLANT IN ANY POSITION

All fruit is offered in bush form which produces its first crop before any other type. As apples, pears + cherries need cross-pollination it is essential to plant two or more varieties of the same fruit unless there are such trees growing nearby.

		Each	Per 3	Per 6
APPLES				
287	Cox's Orange Pippin — the most popular dessert apple	62p	£1.75	£3.40
290	Newton Wonder — Large yellow apple for cooking & dessert in Spring	60p	£1.70	£3.30
289	James Grieve — Early richly-flavoured dessert apple	60p	£1.70	£3.30
288	Golden Delicious — Large yellow dessert apple that keeps well	60p	£1.70	£3.30
CHERRIES				
298	Noble — Large dark red cherry, rich flavour	97p	£2.75	£5.38
297	Napoleon — A sweet juicy yellow-red cherry	97p	£2.75	£5.38
PEARS				
291	CONFERENCE — l.c. and u/s. Self-fertile. A very popular pear with an excellent flavour	65p	£1.85	£3.60
292	Durondeau (DURONDEAU) — A popular sweet + juicy pear	60p	£1.70	£3.30

R.S.A.—INTERMEDIATE 1971

APPENDIX IV

Using one side of a sheet of paper, type a copy of the following Proposal Form. The display should be as indicated.

Caps & centre

Excel Equity Investt Plan - Proposal Form

To: Excel Eq. Fund Managers Ltd., 99 Hall St., Cheapside, Hull, 14.

Title:	Forenames:	Surname:	Née (if married woman):
. . .	. . . .	. . . . . .	. . . . . .
House No. & Street:	**Town:**	**County/Postal Code:**	
. . . .	. . . . . .	. . . . . .	

Length of Plan . . . . years. Guaranteed min.
Sum Assured
(see Table) - . . .

Occupation . . . . Date of Birth . . . . . .
(Birth Certificate shd. be supplied at the outset)

1. Have you ever had (a stomach ulcer), rheumatism, diabetes, tuberculosis, any disorders of the digestive system or kidneys, a growth, or any other such illness? - Yes/No *
2. Has a Proposal on yr life ever been declined, postponed, or accepted on special terms? - Yes/No *
3. Do you engage in any activity or know of any circumstances wh. might affect the risk of an assurance on yr. life? - Yes/No *

* Delete as appropriate. If the answer is "Yes", please give full details on a separate sheet.

Height . . . ft. . . . in.   Weight . . . . st. . . . . lb.
Name & Address of usual Dr. - . . . .
. . . . Known for . . . . yrs.
Date last seen . . . . Reason . . . . . .

I declare that I am in good health & that all the statements set forth are true & complete; I consent to the Company seeking information yf. any doctor who has attended me or yf. any office to wh. a Proposal yf. Assurance of my Life has at any time been made & I authorize the giving of such information.

Dated this . . . day of . . . . . 19. . . Signature of Proposer . . . .

Cheque enclosed (made payable to our Insurance Co., The National Life Office), for the 1st monthly sub. (min. £5).

[£ . . . .]

Returnable in full if you are not accepted.

R.S.A.—ADVANCED 1970

INDEX

A

ABBREVIATIONS
  commercial, 84, 176
  general, 174
  legal, 114, 178
  use of, 4, 6, 7, 31
ABSTRACT OF TITLE, 113
ACCENTS, 102
ACTOR'S PART, 98, 140
ACTS AND SCENERY, 92
ADDRESS
  blocked, 3
  forms of, 170, 180
  indented, 3
  inside, 1, 2, 8, 10, 12, 13, 15, 17, 18, 19
  on envelopes, 22
ADVERTISEMENTS, 49, 52, 140, 141
ADVICE NOTE, 76, 80
AFFIDAVIT, 113
AGENDA
  Chairman's, 118
  general, 117, 118, 140
AGREEMENT, 113
AMPERSAND, 137
APOSTROPHE, 138
APPLICATION FORMS, 51, 52
ASSIGNMENT, 113
ASTERISK, 34, 135
"AT" SIGN, 137
ATTESTATION CLAUSE, 113
AUDIO-TYPEWRITING, 155

B

BACKFEEDING, 163
BALANCE SHEETS, 125, 126, 127, 140
BILL OF QUANTITIES, 123, 124, 140
BODY OF LETTER, 1, 5, 12
BRACE, 135
BRIEF DOCUMENT, 113
BUSINESS LETTERS, 1, 11, 15, 16

C

CARBON COPYING, 143
CARE OF TYPEWRITER, 164
CARET, 135
CEDILLA, 135
CENT SIGN, 135
CHARACTERS AND CAST, 92, 96
CIRCULAR LETTERS, 19
CLEAN DRAFT, 108
COMBINATION SIGNS, 135, 136, 137
COMMERCIAL DOCUMENTS, 75, 140
COMPLIMENTARY CLOSE, 1, 7, 12, 17
CONTENTS PAGE, 47, 48, 49
CONTINUATION SHEETS, 6, 9, 12, 13, 17
COPYING AND DUPLICATING, 143
CORRECTION OF ERRORS, 145, 148, 149, 150, 152
CORRECTION SIGNS
  printers', 28 93
  typists', 28, 32
COUNTERPART, 111
CREDIT NOTE, 83, 140
CUES, 98

D

DAGGER
  double, 34, 135
  single, 34, 135

DASH, 134
DATE IN A LETTER, 1, 11, 13, 15, 17, 18, 19
DEBIT NOTE, 83, 84
DEED, 113
DEGREES SIGN, 135
DELIVERY NOTE, 76, 81
DESIGNATION, 7, 12
DIAERESIS, 135
DISPLAYED WORK, 45
DISPOSITION, 113
DISTINCTIONS AFTER NAME, 4
DIVISION OF WORDS, 6, 132
DIVISION SIGN, 135
DOLLAR SIGN, 135
DOTS
  leader, 48, 58
  on forms, 18, 19
DRAFT COPY, 89, 108
DROPPED HEADING, 89
DUPLICATING
  carbon, 143
  ink (stencil), 143, 146
  offset lithography, 143, 149
  photocopying, 143, 150
  spirit, 143, 148

E

ENCLOSURES, 1, 7, 12, 15, 18
ENDORSEMENT, 111, 112
ENGROSSMENT, 108
ENQUIRY, 75, 76, 77
ENVELOPES
  addressing of, 22
  size of, 141
EQUALS SIGN, 135
ERRORS
  correction of, 145, 148, 149, 150, 162
  types of, 161
EXAMINATIONS
  preparation, 183
  procedure, 184
EXCLAMATION MARK, 135
EXTRA CHARACTERS, 137

F

FAIR COPY, 89, 108
FEET SIGN, 135
FIGURES
  typing of, 29
  use of, 31, 34
FOLDING OF LEGAL DOCUMENTS, 111
FOOTNOTES, 34, 36
FORM LETTERS, 17
FORMS
  filling in, 19
  typing of, 17, 20, 52
FORMS OF ADDRESS, 170, 180
FRACTIONS, 36

G

GRAFTING ON STENCILS, 148

H

HALF-SPACE CORRECTING, 163
HANDBILLS, 50, 52
HANGING PARAGRAPHS, 8, 10, 121, 124
HEADINGS
  centred, 5
  displayed, 45
  in letters, 1, 5, 12
  in manuscripts, 37
  shoulder, 45, 121
  vertical, 68
HOLOGRAPH WILL, 114
HOOK-IN, 102
HYPHEN, 134

I

INCHES, 135
INFERIOR CHARACTERS, 35
INITIALS, 3
INK DUPLICATING, 143, 146
INK RULING

INSIDE NAME AND ADDRESS, 1, 2, 8, 12, 13, 15, 17, 18, 19
INVITATIONS, 52, 54
INVOICES, 75, 76, 82
ITINERARIES, 140, 141, 157, 158

J

JUNIOR, IN ADDRESSES, 4

L

LEADER DOTS, 48, 58
LEASE, 113
LEGAL WORK, 108, 140
LETTERS
 blocked, 8, 9, 13, 16
 business, 1, 11, 15, 16
 composition of, 157
 circular, 19
 form, 17, 20
 indented, 2, 8, 10
 official, 15, 18
 parts of, 1
 private, 15, 17
 semi-blocked, 8, 10, 13
LITERARY WORK, 46, 47, 48, 49, 88, 140

M

MANUSCRIPT WORK, 27
MATHEMATICAL EQUATIONS, 35
MEMORANDA, 21, 140
MENUS, 53, 54, 140
MESSRS., USE OF, 4
MINUTES OF MEETINGS, 119, 120, 140
MINUTES SIGN, 135
MONEY, 133

N

NOTICES, 52, 116, 140
NUMERALS
 arabic, 28, 29, 31, 34
 roman, 28, 31, 138

O

OBLIQUE SIGN, 137
OFFICIAL LETTERS, 15, 18
OFFSET LITHOGRAPHY, 143, 149
OPEN PUNCTUATION, 2, 3, 16
ORDER FORM, 79, 80
ORNAMENTATION, 46, 53, 139

P

PAPER
 sizes of, 67, 140
 types of, 140
 uses of, 140
PARAGRAPH
 block 8, 9
 hanging, 8, 10
 indented, 8, 9
 in letters, 6, 7, 8
 in manuscript work, 28
PARTS OF A LETTER, 1
PER CENT SIGN, 135
PHOTOCOPYING, 143, 150
PLAYS, 92
POETRY, 101
POSTAL CODE, POSITION OF, 4, 23
POSTCARDS, 23, 140
POUND SIGN, 137
PREPARATION FOR EXAMINATION, 183
PRIVATE LETTER, 15, 17
PROGRAMMES, 99, 100
PUNCTUATION
 spacing after, 133
 open, 2, 3, 16

Q

QUANTITIES, TYPING OF, 133
QUOTATION, COMMERCIAL, 75, 78
 in manuscripts, 91
 marks, 91, 137

R

RECEIPT NOTE, 82
RECEIVING DICTATION, 154
REPORTS
  composition of, 157
  typing of, 140
REFERENCE
  books, 158, 168
  in a letter, 1, 12
ROTARY DUPLICATOR, 143, 146

S

SALUTATION, 1, 5, 12, 17, 18, 19
SECONDS SIGN, 135
SECRETARIAL DUTIES, 156
SECTION MARK, 135
SENIOR, IN ADDRESSES, 4
SHORTHAND-TYPEWRITING, 153
SHORT PAGE, 89
SHOULDER HEADING, 45, 121
SIGNATURE, 7, 19
SIGNS
  combination, 135, 136, 137
  correction, 28, 32, 93
SLOPING FRACTIONS, 36
SPACING AFTER PUNCTUATION, 133
SPECIFICATIONS, 121, 140
SPIRIT DUPLICATING, 143, 148
SQUARE BRACKETS, 135
STATEMENT
  commercial, 75, 84, 85
  of claim, 114

STATIONERY, 140
STATUTORY DECLARATION, 114
STENCIL, TYPING OF, 147
SUPERIOR CHARACTERS, 35

T

TABULAR WORK, 46, 57, 140
TAIL-PIECE, 89
TELEGRAMS, 23
TESTIMONIUM CLAUSE, 113
TIME, 133
TITLE PAGE
  of book, 46, 47
  of play, 92, 94
TRANSCRIBING
  recorded dictation, 156
  shorthand notes, 154
TYPEWRITER, CARE OF, 164
TYPEWRITING
  errors, 161
  technique, 161
TYPING FROM DICTATION, 156

U

UMLAUT, 135
UNDERSCORING, 45

W

WILL, 114